BREAKING UP IN BALWYN

A TOAST TO MONEY, MARRIAGE AND DIVORCE

Text by Paul Davies

Photos by Ivan Johnston

Direction by Mark Shirrefs

Produced by TheatreWorks

First performed for the Melbourne Moomba Festival aboard the *MV "Yarra Princess"*

24 February to 24 May, 1983

This book is copyright. Apart from any fair dealing for the purpose of private study, research or review, as permitted under the Copyright Act, no part may be reproduced by any process without written permission. Inquiries concerning publication, performance translation or recording rights should be addressed to the author. Any performance or public reading of *Living Rooms* requires a licence from the author. The purchase of this book in no way gives the purchaser the right to perform the play in public, whether by means of a staged production or a reading.

© The moral right of the author has been asserted.

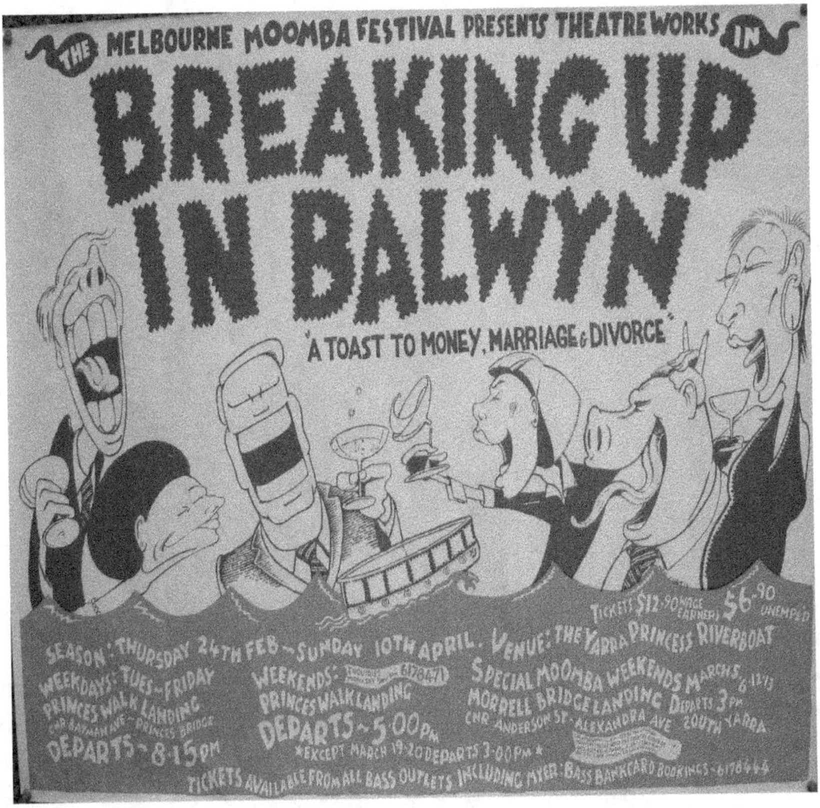

Bringing the World
Back Together

A Picture Play

Volume 4 "*Breaking Up In Balwyn*"
1st Edition Published by Gondwana Press
October 2019
Suffolk Park NSW 2481 Australia

CONTENTS

Cast	6
Location	7
Background and Setting	8

BREAKING UP IN BALWYN
Act One (upstream journey)	**15**
Intermission	**125**
Act Two (downstream journey)	**129**

Critical Reception	267
Illuminators	299
Author	301
Dedication	303

CAST

(left to right)

"Dr." Tamsin Smythe (hydrotherapist) Susie Fraser

Lurlene Fowler ("French maid") Mary Sitarenos

Nigel Davidson (filmmaker) Peter Finlay

Samantha Hart-Byrne (housewife) Hannie Rayson

Michael Hart-Byrne (gambler) Peter Sommerfeld

Snr Const. Lance Tippler (tax squad) Paul Davies

Const. Cathy Waterman (water police) Caz Howard

LOCATION

The play takes place aboard the *MV Yarra Princess*, flagship of Yarra River Cruises fleet, as she motors her serene and regal way along the Yarra River from Princes Bridge in the heart of Melbourne's CBD to a landing four kilometers upstream in the *very eastern* suburb of Toorak - just opposite Herring Island and adjacent to Como Park; one of Melbourne's wealthiest areas.

Here an interval occurs where refreshments are served by Lurlene Fowler, the specially hired Greek "French maid", she is assisted by Samantha's mummy's butler, Kurt. Afterwards the second half of the play unfolds as Samantha's divorce party sails back to the City.

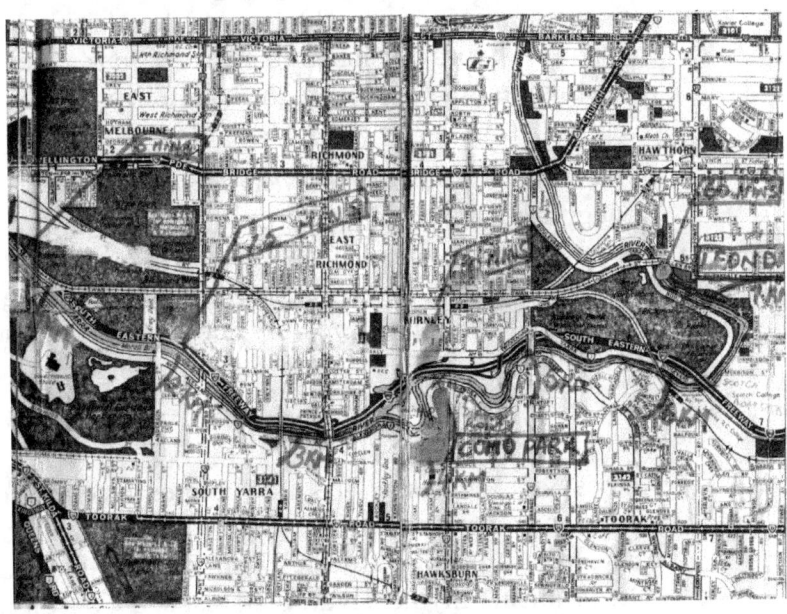

(A working map of the fateful journey
TheatreWorks archive, Fryer Library)

BACKGROUND AND SETTING

It is almost exactly a year since the events known as "*Storming Mont Albert by Tram*" took place. Samantha Hart-Byrne and Nigel Davidson (two strangers who were arrested at the end of that extraordinary tram ride) subsequently spent the night together in a cell in the Balwyn police station. He for possession of a prohibited substance (to wit a cellophane bag containing *cannabis sativa*), she for drunken behaviour. Whilst briefly together and in prison overnight they discovered they had some wonderful mutual interests in common. Interests such as: her money and his talent. This demi-romantic encounter provided the spur that Samantha so desperately needed to throw off her boorish husband Michael Hart-Byrne, a well known tax minimiser and race track "identity". Their marriage had been crumbling for some time. As his gambling and other debts rose, Samantha's hopes and innermost desires sank. The events of that fateful tram ride were the catalyst for real change.

In fact this very morning the *decree nisi* has finally come through from the Family Court and, with Nigel's encouragement Samantha has decided to effectively bury any moral or religious embarrassment about leaving Michael and to, in fact *celebrate* her divorce, embracing her new freedom as an essential and exciting step towards a newer, fuller life.

And as Nigel so wisely, if a little pointedly pointed out: there's no better way for Sam to get "fuller" than have a party. In fact one of her dearest and closest buddies, a "Dr." Tamsin Smythe, Hydrotherapist and Consulting Beautician (tarot readings and relationship breakdowns a specialty) readily approved of the plan and seized upon it as a rare opportunity to solve some of Samantha's associated psychological "issues". (Such as her complete and somewhat mysterious inability to recall any detail of her wedding celebrations to Michael seven years earlier).

Thus, at the Princes walk landing, about 8.15 pm on a weeknight (5 pm weekends) we find 80 or 90 of Samantha's very closest and dearest friends flapping about beside the appropriately named "Yarra Princess" a moderately large Melbourne riverboat.

(photo: TheatreWorks archive, Fryer Library)

Samantha's invite had "implored them all to wear something *outrageous*" which for some of her friends is quite obviously neither difficult nor all that unusual. And as the gay throng waits to board the "Yarra Princess" they are welcomed to the party by Nigel Davidson and Dr. Tamsin Smythe.

NIGEL DAVIDSON 32, is dressed casu-formally in bride-groomish type clothes and wears an unrelentingly bright smile on top of a firm handshake. He greets people familiarly and urges them to sign their names and addresses in a membership book stamped throughout with the title "S & N Blue Light Movie Club". As "guests" readily enough sign his book, Nigel apologizes for the fact that he's got to do this because of the archaic Australian film exhibition regulations. He's dying to show them some of his latest clips as part of the evening's entertainment but in order to do so they just have to "pretend" they're all members of this private film society - just for the night of course. Hardly is the biro dry on the page before he whips the book away and moves in on the next circle of unsuspecting innocents...

Also mingling with the "guests" is TAMSIN SMYTHE, 30. She's introducing herself to various groups as Samantha's "doctor". She thanks them for turning up like this in order to help the poor darling out. Tammy knows it's been a shock to them all to see the traumatic changes in their dear friend, but has high hopes that the river trip will provide the basis for a lasting cure. She squirts them all with a little rosewater and hands them her card:

> **DR TAMSIN SMYTHE**
> Dip. Psych. B. Med.
> Oxon & Bar
> Dip Thong University
>
> **HYDRATHERAPIST AND
> CONSULTING BEAUTICIAN**
> *(Tarot readings and Marriage Breakdowns
> a specialty)*
>
> cheques c/o THEATRE WORKS
> 221 Burwood Highway, Burwood, Victoria.

She tactfully enquires if they have any problems with their relationships and urges them not to hesitate to call her if they *are* experiencing difficulties. She points out (as per the card) that marriage breakdowns are her own particular specialty...

As people move onto the boat they pass a table groaning with presents, at one end of which is a huge, mock wedding cake, several feet high. At the top of this cake a Ken doll (in groom outfit) is stabbing a Barbie doll (bride) in the back. An inscription on the cake reads:

"Samantha and MICHAEL"
1975-1983 r.i.p.
(rest in pieces)

Scattered along the two rows of seats on either side (facing centre) are various fragments of smashed furniture, torn photos, and a defaced wedding album. Attached to this junk - the physical remnants of a collapsing relationship - are tags reading:

> Terra cotta rice bowl (Ming dynasty circa 11th century) flung by M. Hart-Byrne at automatic dishwasher, 24.8.81, after selfish argument about interlocking partnership rights to certain cashable bonds and the BMW.

> Fragments of Queen Anne chair, smashed by M. Hart-Byrne after utterly pointless debate about the need for domestic help.

> Pieces of Mexacala stone figurine (Mesoamerican - proto classic period) used as evidence of mental cruelty

> Aqua lampshade (contemporary Swedish) crushed by a magnum of Glenfiddick held by M. Hart-Byrne

after the share crash of 1973. Note: subsequent mutilations took place after the election of the Labour Government in Victoria, 1982.

Torn Wedding Album (the last straw) We see that MICHAEL's face has been torn from several snaps. In other photos his face is self-obscured by his hat, hands etc. as if trying to hide his identity from court reporters)

At either end of the boat TV monitors are connected to a video tape deck.

DANCE MUSIC playing through the boat's PA system sets the party mood.

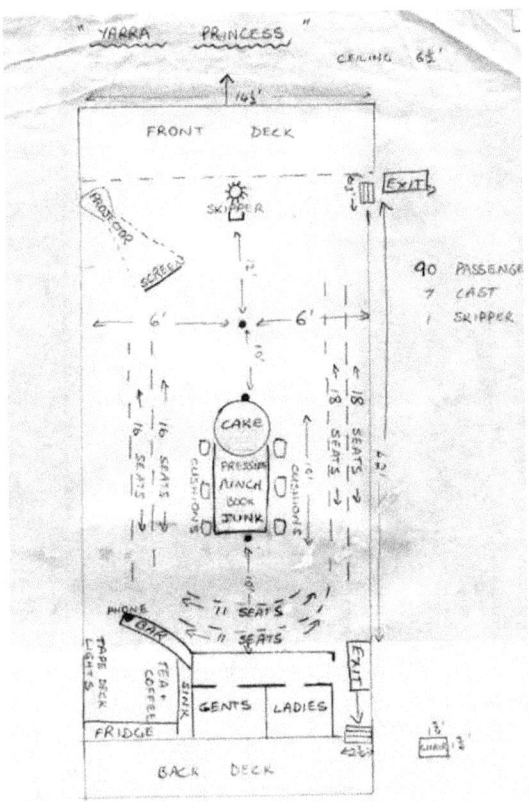

MV *Yarra Princess* floor plan (TheatreWorks Archive, Fryer Library)

ACT ONE
(Upstream Journey)

People coming on board are invited to help themselves to drinks from a generous punch bowl set at the opposite end to the large cake next to a table containing numerous "anti-wedding presents". Here they meet a third character: an ageless woman whose battered cardigan, stockings, sandals, and hairnet, offer a strange contrast to everyone else's smart party gear. This is LURLENE FOWLER. She looks bewildered and out of place as she confronts various gentlemen, and enquires as to whether they "are the boss?" Some may try to ignore her, oblivious to her questioning. Others are unable to help her. Some jokingly refer her to their wives.

Eventually NIGEL and TAMSIN follow the late-arrivers on board. The Skipper revs the engine and the *MV Yarra Princess* starts backing away from the wharf. NIGEL throws a couple of token streamers back at any stranger who happens to be walking past on shore
Then he comes back in and takes the microphone at the front of the boat, beside the Skipper.

NIGEL. Bye! See ya! (waving back out the window to no one in particular)

TAMSIN rushes up to him, agitated.

TAMSIN. Nigel, we can't go yet'.

NIGEL. It's alright, doc, everything's under control.

TAMSIN. But where's the party girl? She's not here.

NIGEL. Don't panic, doc, it's all organised.

TAMSIN. Organised? (cynically) Oh yes, you're so, so. . . inner directed aren't you!

She rushes up the steps of the front door, calling out anxiously towards the shore.

TAMSIN. Samantha?

NIGEL seems totally unfazed, he turns back to his guests and fellow passengers now seated in two rows along either side of the boat. He's trying to put a shine on things in the face of TAMSIN's little outburst. Covering over her irritation with a bright smile.

NIGEL. (tentative) Hi-

ALL. Hi.

NIGEL. How's everybody doing? Good ?

The AUDIENCE nod, generally ANSWERING in the affirmative.

NIGEL. Great? Great. Glad you could make it. Well, welcome everyone to Samantha's little divorce party. *The* Balwyn event of the decade. And Balwyn, as you know, isn't just a suburb - it's a state of mind, right? Right.

Does everybody feel a little Balwyn here tonight? (chuckles).

NIGEL. As you can see, ladies and gentlemen, the *Yarra Princess* has sundered all ties with the land and we are now a free, floating function on the beautiful River Yarra-- or Rivi-era as they say in Niew (sic) Zealand.

He seems to be faultering a little, not quite getting the laughs or the Kiwi accent that he'd been hoping for.

TAMSIN. (impatient) Oh really, Nigel!

NIGEL. (almost like a child) You said I could do my stand-up routine, doctor. You promised.

TAMSIN. Oh yes, yes, alright, if you must, but where's Samantha!?

NIGEL. (back to the crowd) So are we all sufficiently *divorced* from reality yet? Is there anyone here feeling "bound"? Bound down? Part of a married couple? No?

LURLENE. (coming forward) Excuse me - are you the boss?

NIGEL. No. no, Jim's the boss. (indicating the skipper). In fact, I'd like to introduce you to the most important man on board, folks: Jim - our skipper. A truly wonderful human being. His great grandfather was captain of the *Marie Celeste*. His grandfather was captain of the *Titanic*, and his father was captain of the Lower Plenty second eleven. A truly remarkable genealogy.

A few chuckles maybe, but still no laughs. NIGEL
nervously ploughs on, fumbling his notes:

NIGEL. And now, ladies and gentlemen, the moment you've all been waiting for... May I present the most wonderful woman in the world, from Narrak Avenue, North Balwyn - number12, actually, the one with two white tyres on either side of the driveway - no, no, only joking...

LURLENE. (quietly insistent) I'm supposed to report to the lady putting on the party...

But NIGEL continues to ignore her, ploughing straight on...

NIGEL. Yes, ladies and gentlemen, the *new* woman who took the "honey" out of honeymoon and spread it on a "toast" to the bride...Behold! (big gesture, rising in pitch) SAMANTHA - decree nisi - HART-BYRNE!!

And SAMANTHA bursts through the cake, adopting a triumphant pose.

SAM. Hullo! darlings!

There's a big burst of APPLAUSE from the audience

SAM. So glad you could all make it.

NIGEL turns the music up, helps her out of the cake and they gyrate ecstatically around the centre of the boat dancing a wild, improvised tango... Two love birds in constant motion.

TAMSIN stands back from it all looking rather nonplussed as SAM and NIGEL show off their flash-dancing technique. SAM remains distracted by certain "friends" in the audience, turning to each one and greeting them individually.

SAM. Evan, Veronica: simply thrilled to see you, sweetheart.

Hullo Raymond...

Eventually the music fades and the two lovers bring their energetic romp to a dramatic concluding tableau, acknowledging the applause.

SAM. (to NIGEL) Darling, I'm so parched I could drink a Jacuzzi.

NIGEL readily obliges, going to fetch a glass.

NIGEL. A toast, a toast to the new woman.

(handing it to her)

SAM. But nobody's got a glass yet? Where's the maid?

LURLENE gets up and comes forward from her seat down the back.

LURLENE. Ah - so *you're* the boss.

SAMANTHA takes in LURLENE's tawdry, working-class outfit, staggered.

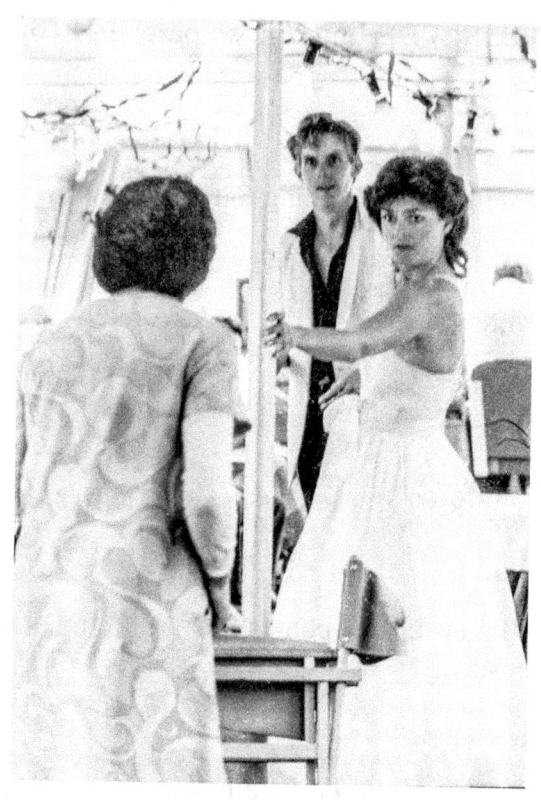

SAM. Ohmygod! Who are you?

LURLENE. Lurlene Fowler's the name. I'm from the agency.

SAM. But I ordered a French Maid.

LURLENE. Sorry, love, all the French ones were booked.

SAM. Good lord!

LURLENE. But me brother's been to Italy...

SAM. Oh...

Realising she's stuck with the woman, SAM sighs and turns to Nigel.

SAM. Nigel, show Mrs. Thingo where to get her cossie.

LURLENE. Fow-ler. Mrs. Fowler. As in "chooks", love.

SAM rolls her eyes.

NIGEL. Right, ah - Mrs. Fowler if could just ask you to walk this way, please.

NIGEL leads her down towards the toilets at the rear of the boat. LURLENE makes an earnest attempt to imitate NIGEL's gait as she follows behind. While SAMANTHA turns back to her guests.

SAMANTHA. Darlings, it's *so wonderful* to be here tonight with all my, very dearest, bestest friends. And I'd like to seize this opportunity to introduce someone so special to Nigel and myself and who, for the past 12 months has taught us how to share, to share things like. . .

NIGEL. (coming back from the toilets) Her bank account and my talent.

SAMANTHA. My money and his problems.

NIGEL. Hey- that reminds me, my wife ran off to Adelaide with my best friend (slight pause). Gee I miss him.

TAMSIN. Nigel - (warning)

NIGEL. No, seriously folks, I used to use clichés all the time. (slight pause) Now I avoid them like the plague.

TAMSIN. I think we can drop the comic role play thank you, Nigel.

NIGEL. (like a small child, pleading) Just one - just one more, doc- I know you'll love it.

TAMSIN realises it's hopeless to try and stop rim now.

NIGEL. How many shrinks does it take to change a light bulb?

TAMSIN. Nigel, I detest the word "shrink" If you'd wanted something in that vein I could have referred you to a witchdoctor.

NIGEL. (persisting) No seriously, how many psychiatrists does it take?

TAMSIN. (giving up, irritated) I haven't the foggiest idea!

NIGEL. Only one - but the bulb has to really want to be changed.

>   NIGEL breaks up at his joke. SAMANTHA too, can't resist a giggle, but TAMSIN remains absolutely deadpan.

TAMSIN. Why don't you just take over, Nigel !? (Waving him on, inviting him in, but assuming he wouldn't dare usurp her role.)

NIGEL. Take over? Right, fine, just take over, just like that…Well take us all here, eh? Take… take my wonderful life partner, Samantha - (slight pause) please… Won't someone take her off my hands (laughs).

>   But even SAMANTHA doesn't find this quite so funny.

SAM. Oh really, Nigel!

>   NIGEL quickly covers…

NIGEL. No - all joking aside (doing his best Lenny Bruce imitation) - I don't know where I'd be without this wonderful woman. Ever since we first met and shared an overnight cell in the Balwyn police station last year - after a regrettable series of events on a tram - she's made me "see" you see. And you know, that's a hell of a thing for an independent Sydney film-maker to do. To "see". Although, of course, I am still committed to the overthrow of the ruling class, I can however, no longer accept the phrase "filthy rich." I mean it's what you *do* with your money that's important. like..."doing" a major feature film on a famous outback crime, but seeing it from different points of view, like... the victim's view, the police view, the aboriginal view...

SAMANTHA. (still smarting from the earlier crack) Oh will you shut-up with that stuff and get on with it!

NIGEL. (genuinely shocked) What? I'm just trying to pitch the plot of my next (film)... their might be other investors (here tonight).

TAMSIN. (stepping in) Yes, as you can see, ladies and gentlemen, Nigel needs help. And yes, I *am* Sam and his and Jim's psychiatrist, or rather, "hydro-therapist" to be more specific. This means that I use water to make people better. No drugs, no expensive supplements, or invasive labotomies. Just plain old H_2O. Now water, ladies and. gentlemen, is absolutely essential to life. In fact two-thirds of every one of us sitting here tonight is made up of water.

SAMANTHA. (coyly) Two thirds of the Yarra is made up of water. (giggles).

TAMSIN. Yes, thank you, Samantha, I'm sure we're all quite aware of the dreadful pollution issues floating all around us, but I also think Nigel's covered most of the comedic entertainment needed for this evening.

SAMANTHA. Oh yes, thank you, doctor. Thank you so much.

(retreating like NIGEL, under her spell, back in her place)

TAMSIN. Now this system - our bodies - like any other system can become "blocked" by certain emotionally traumatic experiences.

NIGEL. (speculating, helpful) Like a kind of...blockage in the s-bend of the mind.

TAMSIN. Quite. and I don't know how many of you Sam has confided in but since she initiated divorce proceedings some 12 months ago she has been utterly, utterly incapable of recalling any aspect of her wedding day.

SAM. Yes-- it's all a blank really. I even have trouble saying the word -"wedd... we...wed... wedd or mar... marr ...marri... marri(age).

NIGEL. It's a most debilitating condition - OHMYGOD!

There's a gasp of horror as Samantha collapses onto the floor.

TAMSIN.(panicking) Don't panic! Don't panic anyone! This is a perfectly normal response to my therapy. Sam's subconscious is just trying to work through a major "block". Ahm...now in order to return her fully to consciousness ah, to get her system flowing again so to speak, I would dearly implore you all to assist me. If you wouldn't mind joining hands and forming a circle to create a whirlpool of healing energy…

> NIGEL goes down the back to offer his body as the link stretching his arms out to unit the two halves of the audience. While JIM spreads his arms to make the connection at the front end of the boat, completing the circle.

TAMSIN. And it's okay, we're not at primary school now, the girls don't have the germs, so it's quite safe to touch them. You'll also notice that JIM has taken his hands off the wheel (to also join in the circle) so we'll have to do this with a certain amount of alacrity…

> TAMSIN takes a large suction device from her briefcase (like something used for clearing drain pipes).

TAMSIN. On the count of three I want us all to say the word "flush" with as much onomatopoeia as possible while I apply the mental enema.

> TAMSIN applies the suction device to SAMANTHA'S prostrate forehead.

TAMSIN. One…two…three

ALL. "FLUSH!"

TAMSIN tugs vigorously on the device and there's a "Pop" sound as it unlocks from SAM's forehead and she immediately springs back to life to much general APPLAUSE.

SAMANTHA. (turning and smiling to somebody nearby) Hullo...

TAMSIN. Oh, well done everybody.

SAMANTHA. Yes. I do feel cleansed. Thank you all ever so much.

There's a faint BANGING SOUND coming from down the back of the boat.

TAMSIN. And thank *you* ladies and gentlemen. Thank you for making your bodily fluids available to us as transmitters of the healing stream. Very generous (of you...)

> The BANGING gets louder, more insistent TAMSIN is forced to break off.

LURLENE. (off) Hey!

TAMSIN. Seems to be a bit of a kerfuffle down the back.

LURLENE. (off) Help. I'm stuck!

SAMANTHA. I think it's Mrs. fowler. She's still in the toilet.

NIGEL. (chuckles) Probably got caught in the chain.

TAMSIN. Well help her out, Nigel, *do* something.

> NIGEL goes down the back to rescue her, pulling the door open.

> LURLENE comes out looking '-very sheepish in a typical "French Maid's" outfit: apron, frilly headband1, black tutu-type mini-skirt, but still with her stockings and sandals on.

LURLENE. Strewth, if Keith could see me now he'd have a heart attack.

TAMSIN. (commanding, impatient) Perhaps we could have the toast, now Nigel.

SAMANTHA. Yes, organise the toast, with Mrs. Fellows will you darling?

LURLENE. (spelling it out) Fow-ler.

NIGEL. Oh - Oh- right...

NIGEL and LURLENE set about the-task of charging everyone's glasses with drinks from the large punch bowl on the central table. While they're thus occupied TAMSIN turns to SAM.

TAMSIN. Time for a little hydra-aerobic tai chi on the front deck, darling.

SAMANTHA. Oh (doubtful) now?

TAMSIN. You've just succumbed to another troubling blackout, dear. We want those nerve endings and all your shakras tingling again don't we?

SAMANTHA. But I don't feel sick, doctor.

TAMSIN. I don't think we should trust our emotions quite that much Samantha. You may not *feel* sick. but I know for a fact that you are.

You are quite ill, my dear. You are far from a well woman.

    And so TAMSIN ushers SAM out onto the front deck.

    While NIGEL remains inside, looking anxious.

NIGEL. (after them) Don't fall overboard (grins) you might dissolve.

TAMSIN. (poking her head back in through the door) That's a good idea, why don't you go through the safety procedures, Nigel. For our guests.

NIGEL. (thinks) Oh - ok, safety procedures, right. . .

    And he fumbles through his collection of audio and
    video cassettes, looking for the one on safety
    procedures while TAMSIN leads SAMANTHA out
    onto the front deck. Here, in full view of her guests
    (and anyone else watching from the riverbank
    TAMSIN takes SAMANTHA through a series of
    hydra-aerobic-tai chi exercises…

While LURLENE continues to charge everybody's glass.

NIGEL has finally located the tape he's been looking for and slips it into the boat's PA system. As a computer-sounding VOICE comes on, NIGEL demonstrates the procedures in the manner of an airline hostess, holding the mask up to his face and so on…

VOICE. Welcome aboard "S&N's Blue Light movie cruise" from Melbourne to Toorak and back. Please observe the exits at the front and gear of the craft (NIGEL indicates) while noting the calm authority my mechanically recorded voice has as it tries not to scare you. As you know, the *MV Yarra Princess* is completely unsinkable (NIGEL stamps the floor with his feet) However, should we in fact meet an iceberg or an old car body and you suddenly find yourself immersed and reacting biochemically with Yarra river water please extinguish all cigarettes. Above all, *do not attempt* to put on any of the life jackets under the benches as they will now be the only things keeping the *Yarra Princess* afloat. (NIGEL takes a life jacket and throws it away). Instead, take an effluent resistor mask (NIGEL takes a mask and puts it on) and place it over the labial and nasal passageways. Then quickly apply eye goggles (does so) ear plugs, rubber gloves and as you float above the waste try to recall some bright happy songs that you might all know together like (sings) "Old man river..." or "We all live in a yellow submarine..." As you wait to be rescued, think of your friends and neighbours floating nearby and try *not* to make waves. Thank you for cruising S & N Blue Light movie cruises.

> NIGEL flicks off the tape and stacks his demonstration gear away as SAMANTHA and TAMSIN swan back in. SAMANTHA flings herself at someone in the crowd.

SAMANTHA. Charles, darling! Hu-llo! Have you got a drink, sweetie?

NIGEL. Yes, I think we might be ready for the toast now.

SAMANTHA. Oh goodie. (turning to address her guests generally) And sorry I was feeling a little overwrought there before... Sorry to have...(passed out like that.)

TAMSIN cuts her off.

TAMSIN. Could everybody be upstanding, please.

SAMANTHA. (Apologetic) This is one of those formal moments-- sorry.

NIGEL. Is there anybody here still married?

There's a few embarrassed chuckles. . .

NIGEL. Well don't worry, you won't feel like it when you get home.

TAMSIN. I'd like to propose a toast, ladies and gentlemen-- to Money:

NIGEL. Marriage!

SAMANTHA. And Divorce!

ALL. To Money, Marriage and Divorce.

LURLENE tries to get the old familiar song going.

LURLENE. For she's a . . .

        For she's a jolly good fel-lowl

        For she's a jolly good fel-low:

And eventually: (with SAM going all uncharacteristically coy and embarrassed)

ALL.   For she's a jolly good fel-low:

                And so say all of us.

                And so say all of us.

                For she's a jolly good fel-el-low:

With excruciating effect, and badly out of tune, LURLENE really holds the note on "and"

LURLENE. AAAAAANN...

ALL. Aaaaaaaaand, so say all of us.

NIGEL. Right if everybody could sink back into ... (realises his mistake) Oh - sorry...

TAMSIN. (warning) NIGEL!

NIGEL. (chastened, he uttered the unmentionable word) ...decline into their seats, please.

SAMANTHA has become quite emotional during the song, brushing away a tear or too...

SAMANTHA. My dear - my very *dearest* friends, it's so thrilling to have you all here tonight on this (breaking down again, going all teary) oh so happy a (crying) on such a happy occasion.

ALL. (sympathetic) Ooooh, Aaaah.

TAMSIN steps forward to put a comforting arm around her.

SAMANTHA. (sniffling into her hanky) I do wish I could enjoy myself again, doctor.

TAMSIN. (patting her arm) There, there, darling...

NIGEL. Enjoy? Hey, I've got an idea.

SAMANTHA. What?

NIGEL. Sam, what do you most enjoy in the world?

SAMANTHA thinks about it. Then the hit on it together:

NIGEL.   ) ____Consumer durables!
SAMANTHA.   )   Consumer durables!

NIGEL. Right. So - why - don't we - open the presents!

SAMANTHA. (thrilled) Oh yes!

TAMSIN. I don't think that's quite right, Nigel...

NIGEL. What?

TAMSIN. You're not supposed to open the presents in front of your guests, it isn't done. You wait till *after* the honeymoon.

NIGEL. What honeymoon? Are you kidding? This is a divorce party!

We can do whatever we like.

SAMANTHA. Hooray!

> SAM and NIGEL eagerly dive into the presents, while TAMSIN stands back, folding her arms, over-ruled for a change. And not liking it one bit.

SAMANTHA. (as she tears at the wrapping paper) Oh I do feel so relaxed tonight, being free of that monster.

TAMSIN. You're not quite free yet of him yet, Samantha - psychologically speaking.

SAMANTHA. But getting most of Michael's money in court this morning - I could have hugged the dear old judge when he gave me all those first recourse debentures in Esanda. *And* the margin loan accounts. You should have seen the look on Michael's face.

NIGEL. I don't think we need dwell on the uglier side of things.

> SAM has opened her first present.

SAMANTHA. (Surprise) oh look, Nigel... (holding it up) from Richard and Liz.

NIGEL. (excited) What is it?

SAMANTHA... Some... (reading the label) deodorant - for you.

NIGEL. (flatly, unenthused) Oh... (then the next one:) Here's something from Dr. Smythe!

SAMANTHA. Oh, Tammy, you shouldn't have...

NIGEL. (holding it, weighing it up) Feels like a book (opens it) Yes, and it's ... (reading the cover, low tone) about having a vasectomy.

> NIGEL slumps. Not the kind of thing he was expecting at all.

TAMSIN. (coy) I do like to give something practical, you know.

SAMANTHA. (amused) I'll make sure he reads it.

TAMSIN. I think Nigel should remain an un-reproduced original.

SAMANTHA. (next one) Oh here's something (reading the card) it's

for both of us, from Mark and Anne (unwraps it) and it's a... (turning to NIGEL) Whip !

SAMANTHA. Oh don't look so gloomy, darling, I promise to use it sparingly (chuckles).

NIGEL. (reading) The card says it's from the U.S. of A...and (brightly) it's from Teddy and Joan! And it's for me... (low) and it's ... some deodorant.

SAMANTHA turns to someone in the audience handing them another present.

SAMANTHA. "Rory", would you like to open this for us, darling?

"RORY" (reading card) to Sam and Nigel...sorry we couldn't make it. leadership struggle keeps us in Canberra, love Andrew and Susan.

"RORY" continues with the unwrapping then hands it over to NIGEL.

NIGEL. (not recognising the present) It's a ... device of some sort...

SAM. It's a suntanning lamp (silly). How lovely. (holding up her left hand) Now I can brown up the spot where my ring used to be.

NIGEL. Here's a little something from Edward and Mrs. Simpson ... and it's. . . some scented soap.

LURLENE. That must be for you, Nige.

NIGEL. How'd you guess.

SAM. Oh Nigel, look - rubies!

> She takes out a ruby necklace, holding it up. There's a lot general "OOOHING" and "'AAAHING

NIGEL. Oh wow! Who's it from?

SAM. (reading the card) "to dearest Samantha. Something to go with your eyes ... (growing anger) red and shiney ... forever, Michael."

TAMSIN.   )
LURLENE.   )------- MICHAEL!
NIGEL.   )

> SAMANTHA rushes to get another present to cover the insult. Ignoring the rubies, casting them aside.

SAM. (brighter) Oh look, here's something else, a little gift, wrapped all in pink, what could it possibly be? It's a. . . (opening it) noose.

NIGEL. (looking down over her shoulder) Who's it from?

SAM. It's for you, darling. From Henry and Anne Boylin.

TAMSIN. But they've been dead for 400 years.

LURLENE. Must be a little joke.

NIGEL. It's a joke alright. I mean look, look at this stuff: Teddy and Joan Kennedy, Richard and Liz Taylor, Andrew and Susan Peacock, Edward and Mrs. Simpson, deodorant, deodorant, scented soap, famous divorces, it's Michael isn't it? It's all his idea of a sick joke.

SAM. How dare he.

NIGEL. Sick, sick.

SAM. (really upset now) He had to do it, you know. Had to get back at me in some silly way. I knew it was a mistake to concede the account at Georges.

NIGEL. He's warped I tell you. Only a diseased brain would go to all this trouble.

TAMSIN. I don't think we should be get too clinically technical at this stage, Nigel.

NIGEL. The furniture, don't forget, he got the furniture too.

SAM. What was left of it.

NIGEL. And little, Sasha.

SAMANTHA starts to break down again.

SAM. Yes. (weeps) He got little Sasha, do we have to relive the whole horror story?

LURLENE. Who's little Sasha?

SAM. My baby.

NIGEL. A hundred a week maintenance was a bit steep.

LURLENE. "Steep"? That's criminal. You shouldn't be paying *him* money.

SAM. I couldn't see Sasha go hungry could I?

LURLENE. You mean he wouldn't feed his own child?

NIGEL. Child? Little Sasha's a Highland Terrier.

LURLENE. Well, a hundred a week. That's a lot of pal.

SAM. Beef stroganoff.

LURLENE. What?

SAM. Sashie's very fussy about her food.

NIGEL. They're probably both settling down to a filet mignon right now.

SAM. I really don't want to think about it now if you don't mind.

TAMSIN. Yes. I agree.

SAM. They might as well auction your heart, because that's the real cost of it. An empty mansion, a BMW, and a broken heart. That's my legacy.

NIGEL. Plus about 3.5 million in fully franked preferential shares.

SAM. Which won't buy me one ounce of happiness.

TAMSIN. Not until you finish your course of aqua therapy.

NIGEL. (handing SAMANTHA another gift) Perhaps this will help.

SAM. From you? oh, darling, what is it?

She opens it, and stares at... a...film can ...

SAM. (perplexed) Wha ?

NIGEL. It's the camera negative from my latest film clip. I'm giving you the rights in perpetuity.

SAM. Nigel! Fancy thinking up such an unusually divine divorce present. (handing it back to him) put it on, sweetheart.

.NIGEL. (modestly) Oh no no- no...

LURLENE. Yeah, give us a squiz, Nige.

NIGEL. Not now, this is Samantha's evening. It's not about me.

SAM. Oh please let them see it, see how marvelous you are.

NIGEL. (all too eagerly) Alright, alright, if you insist. I'll whack the dub on the Akai.

As he goes over to switch on the video cassette deck and insert a VHS tape.

NIGEL. (shyly) It's called "Draggin Me Backwards" - a sort of personal reaction to Queensland.

SAM. (realising) You filmed it on our last trip! Our anti-honeymoon in Noosa?

NIGEL. Yeah, I kept looking at all their so called progress and I thought - this isn't progress, it's more like the middle ages. The place is being run by feudal overlords.

SAM. (Proudly) Isn't he clever?

NIGEL starts the tape.

The film cuts to a shot of the earth slowly turning.

SAM. Oh Nigel - isn't that your film crew?

NIGEL. Yes. The boys did a claret ad at last year's Melbourne Cup.

A fourth title appears: "THEN SUDDENLY IT STOPPED!"

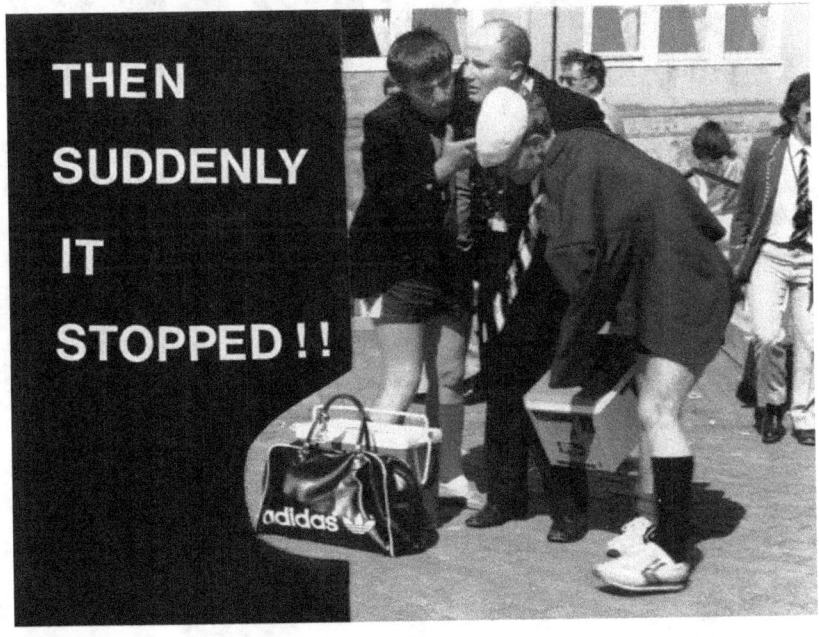

The globe stops. NIGEL's crew stops.

And a fifth title: "AND IN QUEENSLAND IT STARTED TO GO BACK...WARDS."

Brian Eno's *"Draggin' Me Backwards"* plays under the rest of the film where every shot is an image of people or things walking or going backwards including: a giant koala walking backwards up a set of steps…

SAM. Oh look: there's the Giant Koala at Dreamworld!

Other shots of Dreamworld follow: the log ride, the big dipper, shots of crowds, model cars, paddle steamers … all going backwards.

These are intercut with shots that clearly identify parts of Queensland or Brisbane.

LURLENE. Gee it's very creative, it must have cost a fortune to make.

SAM. Yes my chemist was very surprised. We spent more money on film processing than I'd normally spend on cosmetics in a week.

NIGEL. It's not just the physical cost. God! It's the creative energy that goes into it.

NIGEL HUMS along with the music, totally caught up in the magic of his own genius, drawing attention to certain key shots.

NIGEL. Brilliant, wow! Did you see that? The framing's perfect.

It's going on countdown, you know...

> Suddenly we see a shot of CATHY WATERMAN (an old girlfriend of Nigel's). She's walking backwards, then spins round to face the camera, wearing a very fetching dark swimsuit.

SAM. (curious) Who's that, darling?

NIGEL. (a bit too quickly) Just an old friend. (shrugging it off as nothing important).

> Then as a way of distracting attention from CATHY, NIGEL points back to the screen. We see more of the Big Koala, going backwards on the back of big truck, waving at people who themselves are going backwards.

NIGEL. Look there's the Big Koala again. I could watch this for hours.

SAM. It's very compelling, Nigel.

> Over more shots of Queensland, Dreamworld etc:

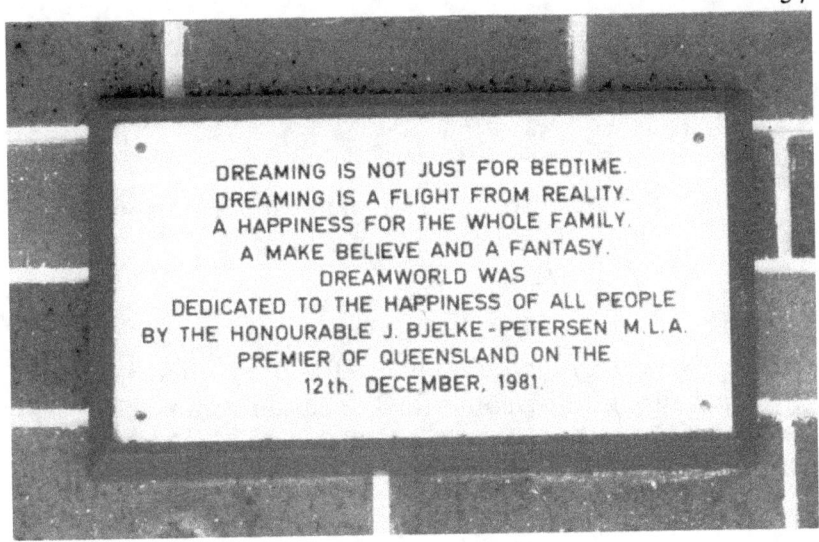

NIGEL. Yes. I find it very moving, I always find my work very ... moving.

SAM. (taking in the audience) It's getting a good response. They're all wrapped.

NIGEL. People love it.

    Suddenly CATHY WATERMAN appears again, side-on, driving a car smiling at the camera.

SAM. (a bit shocked) There she is again!

NIGEL. What? Who?

SAM. That pretty girl. That woman. You've made quite a feature of her haven't you?

> Suddenly we're back looking at other distinctive Queensland icons and places.

NIGEL. I haven't made a feature of her Samantha, they just happen to be some fairly ordinary mid-shots. I probably had them lying around and used them as filler.

TAMSIN. (cutting in) Samantha, is the backwards motion having any qualitative effect on you. Is it triggering any response?

SAM. The sight of that female is triggering a few questions...

> A final shot of CATHY, looking very glamorous an appealing. Almost giving the viewer/cameraman a little bit of a come-on.

SAM. (quite agitated now) Look! There she is again!

> The film ends and NIGEL switches off the player, disgruntled. His moment in the spotlight ruined.

NIGEL. Ohforgodsake, Samantha! It was a long time ago, alright? She was just a *friend*. (making it sound unimportant)

SAM. (with mock patience) Alright, darling.

LURLENE. (quiet aside to one of the guests - but loud enough for all to hear) Didn't think much of that.

NIGEL. I heard that!

TAMSIN. It wasn't so bad, was it?

SAM. (mildly peeved) Well it was a bit literal.

NIGEL. Literal?!

SAM. Yes, I mean, all the backwards thing...

LURLENE. It *was* a bit repetitive.

NIGEL. Repetitive? *All* film's repetitive. I mean it's one frame after another isn't it? That's how projectors work. Haven't you ever heard of the Structuralist Movement?

LURLENE. Nope.

SAM. Nigel's into idiotics, aren't you darling.

NIGEL. (building anger) Semiotics.

SAM. Oh well, semi of one, half a dozen of the other.

LURLENE. What did you think of the fillum, doc?

TAMSIN. Madam, I was totally underwhelmed by it.

NIGEL. Thanks a lot. You're supposed to be *boosting* my confidence.

LURLENE. How many fillums have you made, Nige?

SAM. It's not quantity we're interested in here, it's quality.

NIGEL throws a long soulful look into the bottom of his glass. Takes a deep breath.

NIGEL. I'll have another large-ish gin sling thanks, Mrs. Fowler.

LURLENE. (looking around for other directions) What now?

NIGEL. Yeah, yeah, now - if you wouldn't mind. Now, and later, and one after that.

SAM. And a tiny bacardi daiqueri, thank you Mrs. Fowler - with just a touch of vermouth.

LURLENE. Wee wee, boss.

LURLENE looks at the spirit bottles (near the punch bowl) rather uncertainly. She recognises the gin, opens it, takes a glass.

LURLENE. One gin sling and dakery coming up.

Trying to imitate a proper "bartender" she kind of throws the gin across from the bottle to the glass, missing by miles and spilling half of it onto the floor. She wipes the fluid off her sandshoes by scraping them on her calf muscles and sloshes Vermouth and some spirits around in a cocktail shaker to make the "Daiqueri".

Then, as if to cover over her ineptitude (while SAM and NIGEL share an eye-rolling moment):

LURLENE. So *how* many fillums have you made, Nige?

NIGEL. Too many.

LURLENE. How many?

NIGEL. Well, alright, I've made a few, alright? (little cross)

LURLENE. A few ? (handing them their drinks)

NIGEL. Yeah - a couple of clips, a couple of home movies...

LURLENE. (surprised) Home movies! And you're going to try make it as a professional are ya, love?

NIGEL. (proudly) I *am* a professional, I *never* work for nothing. Of course, I may not have made a *fortune* exactly, but now, with Sam's help...

LURLENE. But I mean you're going to make a real fillum - like what they call a feature fillum?

NIGEL. I'm in the drafting stages - yes.

SAM. The industry *needs* people like Nigel. He's different. He's fresh.

LURLENE. Not if all that deodorant's any guide.

SAM. Show them, darling, screen the work that you've already made - let your films speak for themselves. Let your spirit soar.

NIGEL. (his-confidence dented a bit) No- I don't ... (think so...)

TAMSIN. Nonsense.

NIGEL. I don't think it's the right atmosphere.

SAM. Did Hitchcock, did Kawasaki worry about "atmosphere"?

NIGEL. It's ... it's not ready yet.

TAMSIN. Nigel, this is no time to get artistic cold feet. Show us your anti-honeymoon film at least. It might even be useful.

NIGEL. Look, how would Spielberg have felt if "*ET*" was shown as a rough cut?

SAM. He's so shy, poor darling._

NIGEL. Samantha, I'm not shy, ok?

SAM. Sweetie, it's a wonder you've got has far as you have in such a public, out-there industry. You can't go hiding your light under a bushel.

TAMSIN. (sensing another area of healing opportunity opening up) Do you have a problem with the word, "shy", Nigel?

NIGEL. (yells) I SAID I'M NOT SHY, ALRIGHT! (sobering a little, lowers his voice) I don't have any problems with it, (shaking, holding himself tightly) thank you, doctor.

TAMSIN. Well show us the film, then.

NIGEL It's my baby, it's not ready to be born yet. she moves towards the video.

TAMSIN makes a move towards the video player.

TAMSIN. I'm not o going to stand here talking to a petulant child.

NIGEL intercepts her, and grabs the tape before she can insert it and rushes over to the open doorway, holding it out over the water, threatening to drop it.

NIGEL. I'd rather see it dissolve in the Yarra than have it play unfinished.

TAMSIN moves smartly over to him and slaps his face, takes the tape back off him.

TAMSIN. Now sit down and say 65 times "I must not annoy my therapist if I want to get better."

66

NIGEL looks-deeply-shocked, hanging there in the doorway, holding his face.

TAMSIN moves back inside and starts the tape.

TAMSIN. Now, Samantha, this is the film NIGEL made of your little love nest in Noosa. I want to use this film as an emotional trigger.

SAM. (thrilled, excited) Oh lovely.

TAMSIN. I want to jog your memory back to that first honeymoon with Michael. . .

The first title comes up on screen: "NOOSA ANTIMOON":

Then the second: "UNE FILME DE NIGEL DAVIDSON"

Then the third:

The next shot is of a car driving through the rain.

SAM. They call it the sunshine coast, but really, it rained the whole time we were there.

There's another shot of "The Big Cow" as we drive past it in the rain.

SAM. Oh there's the big cow! (giggles) There's a little milk bar inside its tummy.

Other shots follow the Big Pineapple, The Big Bottle etc...

TAMSIN. Relax, breathe through it, free associate...

SAM. You'd like Queenslanders, doctor, they've obviously got a "giant" complex.

> Sam is enjoying this now. Amused at her pun.

TAMSIN. (still probing) Did Michael have a giant complex?

> We see shot of Noosa's main street, seen through the glass of a lift going down the outside of a large building.

SAM. There's Hastings street!

TAMSIN. Go with the flow (like she's conducting an orchestra) Take it

deeper, deeper...

SAM. (misunderstanding she just deepens her voice) Oh I'll never forget my weekend in Noosa.

TAMSIN. (quickly) Why?

> Now a shot of a couple walking along Noosa's main beach.

SAM. (still in a deep voice) It was so romantic. (then lighter, with excitement) That's me! We got a Japanese couple to take that one.

> Close on a copy of the book "*Life After Marriage*" and widen to see NIGEL and SAM reading it on a beach. Then a tilt up an enormous block of luxury units.

SAM. Oh - here's the block of units I got off Michael in court this morning.

> Close on the architectural plans for another tall building.

SAM. And there's daddy's block. His isn't quite finished yet. He's selling off the plan.

NIGEL. (cynically) "Off the planet" if you ask me.

TAMSIN. (warning) Nigel.

> A tilt down a motel block called "The Breakers".

SAM. Oh - there's "The Breakers". We stayed there too. I'm at the bottom of this shot aren't I darling?

But at the bottom of the shot we see that's it's CATHY WATERMAN again, waving back at the camera.

SAM. Who's that?

LURLENE. That's that pretty girl again.

NIGEL. (quickly) I'm sorry there's been some mix-up in the editing.

TAMSIN. Nigel, we don't want to upset Samantha, do we?

NIGEL. I told you the film wasn't finished. I tried to warn you:

We're inside "The Breakers" now. Shots of rain on the windows, a luxurious lounge room.

We pan over plates of oysters, mud-crabs, croissants...

TAMSIN. (trying to distract SAM away from the mix-up) Oh look, that's your breakfast isn't it? Looks delicious.

Then a shot of a bottle of champagne being opened. A woman's hands struggle with it, she eventually she uses a fork to wedge the cork open.

SAM. They're not my hands. (rising indignation) I'd never open champagne with a fork!

TAMSIN. (quickly trying to deflect her concern) Champagne, oysters, your anti-moon breakfast...

NIGEL. Look, there we are again see...

> Back to a shot of SAM and NIGEL on a beach, all cuddly and loving. But the camera tilts up and we see a factory in the background, then the West Gate Bridge.

LURLENE. That's not Noosa, that's Port Melbourne!

NIGEL. (covering quickly) Well I had to shoot a few close-ups back here to give the thing some pace.

> There's a pan round the luxury bedroom, things are a bit of a mess.

TAMSIN. Oh look, here you are the morning after, disheveled,

in bed, happy.

> The camera moves in on a sleeping figure partly obscured by blankets, slowly the cameraman (NIGEL) pulls the blankets back to reveal: a sleeping CATHY WATERMAN!

SAMANTHA is on her feet.

SAM. Stop! Stop the film!

A quick shot of NIGEL on the beach, he is running towards the camera, putting up a hand in protest.

NIGEL. (on film) Samantha, wait - don't stop the film! Samantha! Don't turn it off!

But SAMANTHA continues to storm towards the video machine, stabs at the "off" button.

The screen goes blank. SAMANTHA is livid.

NIGEL. There must have been some mix-up with the neg matching.

SAM. How dare you!

TAMSIN. You've sabotaged my therapy with your incompetent, Casanova exploits.

NIGEL. Look, it was a long time ago._

SAM. You took *her* on *my* anti-honeymoon.

NIGEL. Samantha, just don't try to run my life or tell me how to write my films, ok?

SAM. Well, don't tell me how to write the cheques then.

That stabs home.

NIGEL. What?

SAM. I can almost accept it being a long time ago, but did they all have

to be such adoring shots (shakily pouring herself another hefty gin).

NIGEL. They weren't adoring shots, they were fairly ordinary mid-shots. Almost boringly ordinary. I told you it wasn't ready to be seen.

SAM. Tamsin was right - you're so *tight*, Nigel. You, you ... (lunges at him, pummeling his chest with her fists) I could-kill-you!

TAMSIN. Darlings, you can't fight here, this is a divorce party!

SAMANTHA settles a little, trying to compose herself.

SAM. Alright, I got one from Michael, now I want one from *him*.

NIGEL. You cant divorce me - we're not even married, remember.

SAM simmers for a moment or two.

SAM. Somehow I don't think *"Desperate Convictions"* is going to work as a film, anyway.

NIGEL. How can it fail? It's got Brian Brown, it's got camels...

SAM. My money.

NIGEL. My talent.

SAM. We haven't seen much evidence of that have we? 'Lot more going to the beach than writing.

NIGEL. I keep telling you: it's the conceptual phase. I *think* while I'm swimming, I *think* while I'm riding my bike, I *think* in the beer garden.

NIGEL's bleeper goes off.

LURLENE. I think you're wanted on the phone.

NIGEL goes to answer it.

NIGEL. (querying JIM) Has this got an ISD facility?

LURLENE. Well it hasn't got a cord.

JIM nods. Nigel starts dialing.

SAM. Who are you ringing?

NIGEL. It's the call from Singapore.

NIGEL dials about 15 digits, waits a moment.

NIGEL. Tan? Nigel. Speak to me babe ... (listens) uh huh. . .(shocked) What? Look, don't, give me that stuff about buyers market, man, do what everybody else does! Acquire a shelf company without any profit components and borrow the extra. You can consolidate the losses and leverage a loan then claim the interest on your tax.

SAM. Nigel, what is going on?

He holds an hand up, urging her to wait.

NIGEL. Of course we've got completion guarantees.

SAM. Nigel?

NIGEL covers the phone.

NIGEL. The mini-golf link at Surfers just isn't shifting.

SAM. But that's prime real estate. It's worth a fortune.

NIGEL signals her to hold it, listens back into the phone.

NIGEL. Look, we're hanging on 158 Ks for that block, Tan, that's bottom line, man.

SAM. At least, at least 158 thousand.

NIGEL. What? (flabbergasted) Thirty two? ... Thousand? (immediately) we'll take it.

SAM. (appalled) What?

NIGEL. You owe me one, Tan. (hangs up)

SAM. It's out of the question, Nigel. That's giving it away.

NIGEL. (sighs) Look it's only script development money. I can squeeze out at least a treatment on that much.

SAM. That land has doubled in value in the last two weeks. This is Surfers Paradise we're talking about.

NIGEL. Look, if I push myself, I might even be able to manage a whole scene breakdown. We'll use the canal development money for the full draft.

SAM. (ordering) MICHAEL! Ring Tan back and call the whole thing off.

She goes to dial the phone, NIGEL catches her wrist. Glaring straight at her.

NIGEL. What did you call me?

Egged on by LURLENE the guests react with mock admonition.

ALL. Ooohuuuah!

SAM stops, trying to focus on the present again. Massaging her temples slightly.

This curative party idea of TAMSIN's isn't quite having its expected healing effect.

Meanwhile the MV Yarra Princess approaches a very odd looking prospective passenger:

While back on the boat, drama unfolds:

SAM. I know what I'd like to call you.

TAMSIN. (eager, sensing a turning point) Yes, Samantha, go on, say it...

SAM. That's the most pathetic deal-making performance I've ever seen.

NIGEL. (a really sore point) Did you call me MICHAEL!?

SAM. It must have been a Freudian slip.

But before it can get any worse between them
LURLENE suddenly notices the rather bizarre figure
waiting on the shore.

LURLENE. By jeeze, what's that!?

SAM. (vaguely following her look) What, what is it, dear?

LURLENE. There's some kind of big hairy thing over there, on the shore. . .

They glance across at a "monster" sitting casually by the shore under an old umbrella.

The boat's lights blink and off, then go out. Adding to growing alarm.

TAMSIN What? what's happening?

However NIGEL is still totally caught up in his own problems.

NIGEL. Look, doc, I don't think the amnesia recovery plan is working, you know?

LURLENE. (still gawking at the shore) Is that for *real*?

TAMSIN. (to NIGEL) Whatever are you talking about?

> Conversations start to overlap as the confusion and the panic builds.

NIGEL. This whole mock-wedding thing to get Samantha's memory back. It's just not the full quid, is it?

TAMSIN. Nonsense, Nigel, it's working fine.

SAM. (still looking through the boat's window) Oh look it's a giant floppy muppet of some kind. How quaintly silly.

> We hear the engine cut out, the lights blink on and off again. And stay off.

LURLENE. (starting to panic) Wha... What's happened to the engine?

SAM. How delightfully Moomba. I do think Moomba adds so much life to the city, don't you?

NIGEL. (following TAMSIN, unable to let go) I feel ...(taking off his bow tie) I just don't feel like a de facto groom that's all.

SAM. Whatever are you talking about Nigel?

NIGEL. I feel more like the worst man, you know (breaking down a little) If the best man gives the bride away then the worst man takes her back. Well that's me, Nigel Davidson, w... w... w... w... (shaking again, stuttering) worst man. I copped the bride and ah, I'm stuck with her.

SAM. (savaging him) It's the *father* of the bride who gives the bride away, you blithering idiot!

NIGEL is stunned.

NIGEL. Wha? What did you call me?

LURLENE. (back at the monster) That's no muppet, That's something horrible that's broken loose from the zoo.

SAM. (attention back to the shore) What?
s

LURLENE. It's some-kind of furry animal with big, white teeth.

NIGEL. Did somebody call me an "idiot" just then?

TAMSIN. It's a bit far south for a polar bear don't you think?

But the panic continues to build throughout the boat.

LURLENE. Yuk. It's got claws and everything.

NIGEL. Listen, doc, I just don't feel very secure at the moment, would... would you mind if I expressed a little tension?

SAM. (panics) We....we're drifting, why are we drifting?

TAMSIN is going for the door, she needs to escape, but NIGEL is close behind her.

TAMSIN. Nigel, you've been primalling far too much lately.

NIGEL. (begging) J...j... j... j ... just a little one?

SAM. Primalling? It's not the shouting, it's the drinking that's giving him the shakes.

TAMSIN. How many times have you primalled this week, Nigel?

NIGEL. Si-si-si…

But LURLENE remains focused on the shore.

LURLENE. oh no. . .

NIGEL. Si…si…si…

The *Yarra Princess* drifts into the jetty and the "monster" jumps aboard.

LURLENE. It's a full blown ...

NIGEL. Si... si... si...si... si

NIGEL's primal scream coincides with everyone else's.

NIGEL.)   Sssssiiiiiiixxxxxxxx!

LURLENE.)Monssssstttteerrrrrrr!

SAM.)   Aaaaaaaaaahhhhhhh!

TAMSIN.)   Aaaaaaaaaahhhhhhh!

LURLENE. The lights, the lights, switch on the lights!

Pandemonium breaks loose as the gorilla/monster chases various apoplectic characters around the boat.

LURLENE is groping for the lights but by accident she hits a button that starts a strobe. This accentuates the terror. The monster bear-hugs various people and the panic builds. NIGEL is reaching for effluent resistor masks and various floatation devices.

NIGEL. Abandon ship! Abandon ship!

But eventually somebody, probably JIM, finds the right switch and the lights come back on. The monster freezes in front of LURLENE who has managed to gather the whip from the presents table and is forcing him slowly back. Threatening with the whip.

LURLENE. Back. . . back.

The panic slowly subsides as the monster backs away from LURLENE. "He" holds up a piece of paper, waving it, like a surrender flag.

MONSTER. (mumbling) Bluminable Nogrum ...

NIGEL. What?

SAM. What?

TAMSIN. What?

LURLENE. He's trying to say something.

MONSTER. Nits uh bluminable nogrum.

LURLENE. (brightens) He says he's an "ab-om-ina-ble snow-gram"

NIGEL. I think she's got it. By George she's got it.

SAM. I didn't know you could speak yeti, Mrs. Fowler.

LURLENE. Oh you pick up quite a lot of different tongues down St. Kilda way. It's a very cosmopolitan suburb you know.

TAMSIN. What on earth's an "abominable snowgram"?

LURLENE. You know, it's like a singing telegram, or a gorilla-gram. We had one at Meryl's 21st.

MONSTER. (muffled mumbling nodding). Mmm...Mmm

SAM is thrilled.

SAM. What a simply spiffing idea. I wonder which one of my dear zany friends thought up such a fab party joke? (to an audience member) Was it you, Ewan ?

MONSTER. (holding up the telegram) Mead it genow?

LURLENE. I think he wants to read it now.

SAM. Oh yes please.

The MONSTER reads and LURLENE translates

MONSTER. Nememba dah moatshed ack n nevety du...

LURLENE. Remember the boatshed back in '72 ...

MONSTER. Nen ioletz ur ed, nd oses er ue ....

LURLENE. When violets were red and roses were blue...

MONSTER. Erds at ere ed utween mie and oo.
        Erds at i ed at ever er ue...

LURLENE. Words that were said between me and you
        Words that I read that never were true

MONSTER. Hen erds uv nanga ow ery erst loo
                   Huh elesie wilds nd its ike a hoo…

LURLENE. Then words of anger our very first blue
                   The jealousy builds and fits like a shoe…

MONSTER. Ow erds utween uz ah oar to ew
                   Ut memba the oatshead aie sertenlie do.
                 Hen fecshun as anish ike da ornung ewe.

LURLENE. Now words between us are far too few
                 But remember the boatshed I certainly do-
               When affection has vanished like the morning dew.

    Finally NIGEL can take it no longer.

NIGEL. Who *is* this lu-lu?

    He strides over and tugs at the MONSTER'S head piece, pulling it off…

    Revealing:

SAM. MICHAEL!!

TAMSIN. It's you!!

MICHAEL smiles mischievously.

MICHAEL. Yes hullo everyone, pleased to meet you (shaking hands with a stranger) Michael Hart-Byrne. Mike...

NIGEL. Look, buddy, why don't you just take your animal suit and go.

MICHAEL. (turning to her) Samantha! You look radiant dear - did something run at the laundromat?

SAMANTHA. Somebody's put you up to this at the *Cricketer's Arms* haven't they?

MICHAEL. (holding out his hand to Nigel) Neville, how nice

to see you again.

NIGEL. I find that offensive. (refusing to shake Michael's outstretched hand)

SAMANTHA. Get out! Get out of my houses.

MICHAEL. (perfectly reasonable) It's not your house, dear, it's a boat I'm afraid.

SAMANTHA. Rented with my money.

MICHAEL. Stolen from me by your unscrupulous QC this morning.

SAM. I needed *help*, Michael (breaking down again), and you refused to budge, refused to even listen! I mean it's a huge house. It takes an absurd amount of cleaning just to keep presentable.

MICHAEL. You had every conceivable electrical device the Japs have thought of.

NIGEL. (intervening between them) Look, this, isn't some sort of office grog-on, or Rugby party, you know, you-just can't come gate-crashing in here.

MICHAEL. (gesturing around) Are you kidding, Neville, I owned most of this stuff here, won half of it at Flemington on a couple of trifectas.

NIGEL. The name's NIGEL! (threateningly).

MICHAEL. Yes, well that figures...

TAMSIN. You see, Samantha, through divorce private emotions are often translated into money or things. Now a final confrontation about possessions is part of the healing psychological process.

SAMANTHA. (suddenly accusing TAMSIN) How dare you go to these lengths (indicating MICHAEL) to try and *jolt* me into remembering.

TAMSIN. (innocently) I had nothing to do with his arrival.

MICHAEL. (to TAMSIN) you're not still trying to get her to remember it, are you?

TAMSIN. And I was experiencing some degree of success until you burst in.

SAMANTHA. Tamsin, this is a very poor joke.

TAMSIN. Darling, I never joke.

MICHAEL. That's certainly true - a halfway decent smile would crack her make-up wide open.

TAMSIN glares at him with a look of pure fury. But she's immediately distracted by SAMANTHA again breaking down.

SAM. It's my therapy and *I'm* going to control it.

TAMSIN. Darling, it's your party and you'll cry if you have to.

SAM. I'll cry if I want to.

LURLENE. (to audience) You would cry too, if it happened to you.

MICHAEL. Oh god!

TAMSIN rounds on MICHAEL eying him narrowly.

TAMSIN. (then circling him, going into clinical mode) I wonder where this fixation with costumes comes from,

Michael, did you ever find yourself dressing up in your mother's furs as a child?

MICHAEL. I came as a monster, Tamsin, because that's how she (indicating SAM) tells it... And I can't understand it, because, really I'm a just a pretty wonderful guy all round when you really get to know me. Ask my friends.

SAM. I wish I'd never marr . . . marrie. . . ma ...

TAMSIN. (encouraging) Yes, yes, use it, go on, say it!

SAM hangs there with her mouth open, twisting around the word "married" ... but eventually gives up.

SAM. I can't.

TAMSIN. Of course you can't, that's why I'm here. That's why you *need* me. (peremptorily) So what do you say?

SAM. (meekly, under her spell again) I'm sorry, doctor.

TAMSIN. Sincerely sorry?

SAM. (nods, contrite) Sincerely sorry.

TAMSIN. Good, now we can get on with the party. Could we have the next film, please, Nigel?

NIGEL. (slight alarm) What, now?

TAMSIN. I know it wasn't planned like this, but we have no choice with him (MICHAEL) here now. In fact it might even be useful.

NIGEL. Oh alright. It's not my film anyway.

NIGEL goes to start the video cassette recorder.

MICHAEL. How can you flaunt the collapse of our happy relationship like this?

TAMSIN.(mocking) Happy? Relationship? Michael, it was nothing more than a debased entanglement from which Samantha is still painfully attempting to extricate herself. . . (turning back to her) I want you to concentrate. . .

TAMSIN places SAMANTHA in a chair in full view the video screen and squirts her with a little rosewater.

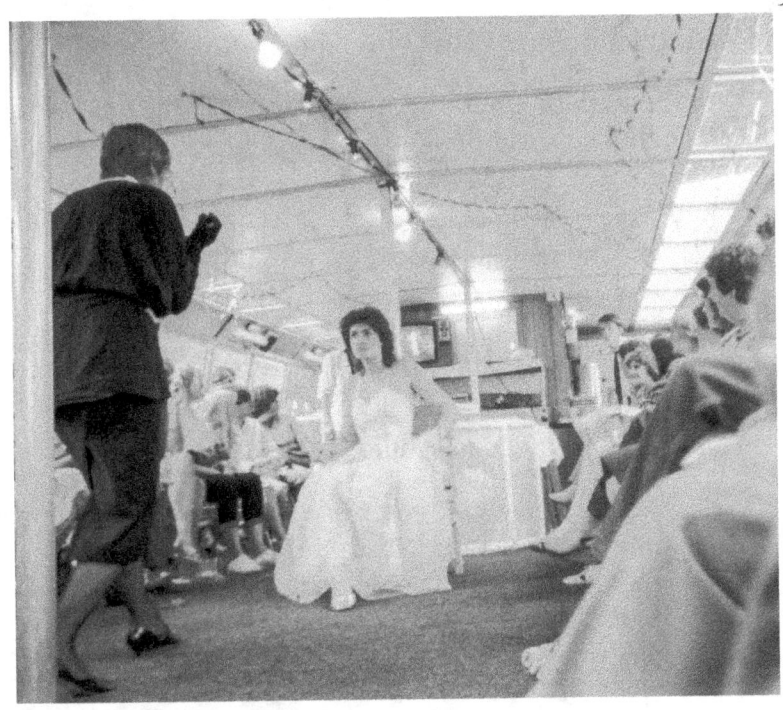

SAM. (uneasy with Michael still there) Do I have to do it in front of him?

TAMSIN. I'm afraid, at this stage, it's either break through or break down, dear.

Nigel starts the video and it's all shot home movie-style as SAM comes out of Daddy's mansion and hops into the Rolls while a chauffeur holds the door open.

TAMSIN. I want you to remember ... to remember a certain day in late 1975.

SAM. (closing her eyes) November, November the 11th, yes

(then opens them, up at the screen) Oh look! There's Daddy's house in Toorak.

TAMSIN. (quickly) Do you remember it?

SAM. (pause) No.

As the Rolls drives on we see Sam and her father pass an old drunk on the street. From the footpath going past he urges her "not to do it." We see also various louts driving past,

shouting out, beeping the Rolls, making lewd comments...

LURLENE. Doesn't she look be-ewdiful...

MICHAEL. Are we supposed to be taking this seriously?

TAMSIN. Will you shut-up, Michael.

Then a shot of MICHAEL in a dinner suit, getting dragged along to the church by a Mafiosa figure wearing dark sunglasses and carrying a violin case.

SAM. There's Michael with his best man.

MICHAEL. Ah yes (coyly), Shifty. My accountant.

SHIFTY pushes MICHAEL up the steps of the church, MICHAEL is trying to hide his face with his hat and grip onto anything that will hold them back.

TAMSIN. (dropping in again) Do you remember him, Samantha?

SAM. How could I, I haven't arrived yet.

Fair enough. Tamsin backs off, the wedding film rolls on:

As SHIFTY continues to push MICHAEL on into the church, the reluctant groom seems to be reaching out to grab onto anything that might hold him back.

At last we see shots of SAMANTHA arriving in the Rolls Royce.

LURLENE. (brightly) Ah, there you are.

SAM's small scotch terrier, SASHA, happily rushes up to the car as the resplendent bride exits and adjusts her flowing veil prior to entering the church.

SAM. (brightly) Oh, look, there's little Sasha.

Suddenly DADDY lashes out with his boot at the dog shooing him away.

SAM. Oh No! Daddy's trying to kick him!

We cut forward to the bridal party coming out of the church everybody throwing confetti, applauding, happy.

Except for MICHAEL who is again being dragged along by his forbidding looking accountant.

SAM. Oh look, Michael, there's Shifty. Your accountant.

Excited, SAM spots various people in the crowd.

SAM. There's mummy and daddy, and Karl, and Sky and Gabriel...

TAMSIN. Do you remember them?

SAM. Of course (silly), they're my family.

TAMSIN. (specifically) Do you remember them at the wedding.

SAM. (pause, sadly) No-

106

    We see other shots of the reception, champagne being popped, little Sasha bouncing around everyone's ankles.

    NIGEL. God marriage is a farce isn't it ?

    LURLENE. No it isn't, Keith and I are very, very happy.

    Other shots of the reception lead to the compulsory photos in the park:

    With all the relevant family groupings:

SAM. Mummy and Daddy Again!

SAM. (spotting little SASHA again) Oh there's my little baby, isn't he

gorgeous...

The final shots of the wedding home movie are of MICHAEL and SAMANTHA driving off.

MICHAEL. Samantha dear, there's something I have to tell you...

TAMSIN. Not now, Michael.

MICHAEL. I think she should know.

TAMSIN. (warning) MICHAEL!

SAM. (curiosity piqued) Know what?

MICHAEL. It's about little Sasha.

SAM. He's getting his cheques isn't he?

MICHAEL. Yes, I've opened an access account in his name. But it isn't that...

TAMSIN. (butting in) Did the film trigger any faint stirrings of memory, Samantha?

> But of course by now SAMANTHA is totally preoccupied with little Sasha

SAM. What is it, Michael, what?

> MICHAEL takes her hand, preparing her for a shock.

MICHAEL. Sam, I have to tell you... little Sasha has a pulmonary embolism.

SAM. (shocked, staggered) Oh NO! (then) What's that? Exactly.

    SAM looks panicked.

MICHAEL. His little heart is about to erupt out of his rib cage, dear.

(quickly) But it's ok - there's a cardiologist in LA. He says there's a fifty/fifty chance... but he's hopeful that a coronary bypass may take most of the pressure off.

    Throughout the ordeal of the wedding film NIGEL has become more and more restive, finally he can stand it no longer.

NIGEL. LA! What's wrong with a vet in Balwyn?

SAM. (rounding on him) Oh you beast, what would you know?

MICHAEL. So you see, I...I need two first class tickets to the west coast.

SAM. Yes, yes of course, I'll give you my Pan Am card. Does it have to be open heart surgery?

MICHAEL. Yes, and I'm afraid the hospitals in America... (shrugs knowingly, hands widening)

SAM. Everything, I'll pay for everything. He's got to have the best, Michael, I'm counting on that. Nothing but First Class ...

MICHAEL. Just get your cheque book out, dear.

SAM. Nigel, can you pass it to me.

NIGEL. You've got to be joking!

SAM. (commanding) NIGEL! Give me my cheque book!

> That' an order. So reluctantly NIGEL takes the cheque book from inside his coat pocket and hands it to her.

> MICHAEL turns to some people nearby in a smug aside, raising an eyebrow.

MICHAEL. Round one.

> NIGEL can't believe it.

SAM. (poised with biro over cheque book, ready to write) How much to you need, Michael?

MICHAEL. Just make it out for a great deal of money, dear.

NIGEL. Great deal of money! Fantastic. There goes Brian Brown, there go the camels.

SAM. I didn't know you cared, Michael, I thought he was just a dog to you.

MICHAEL. (greasily sincere) Little Sasha's not just a dog, Samantha, he's more a way of life. I love little Sasha.

SAM. How much, Michael?

MICHAEL. What dear, love or money?

TAMSIN. It's not little Sasha, it's little Samantha I'm worried about.

MICHAEL. I'm sorry to, you know, interrupt the party like this... but -

TAMSIN. You've utterly demolished my therapy at its most crucial stage!

SAM. It's alright, Tamsin, I'm never going to remember it. My only regret is... I never really got to know you did I, Michael (nostalgic, dreamy, sentimental)

SAM's mellowing towards MICHAEL is really putting NIGEL on the boil.

SAM. You're feelings were always so... so private.

NIGEL. That's because he kept them in a safe deposit box at the ANZ bank.

SAM. NIGEL, you're such a porpoise sometimes. Why don't you go and put some music on. It's so stuffy in here, if I don't kick. up my heels soon I think I'll suffocate.

NIGEL reluctantly swallows his pride and goes to start the tape.

MICHAEL. You don't think the significance of this boat trip has escaped me do you? The symbolism of it?

SAM. What?

MICHAEL. You, on this boat, sailing upstream to rid yourself of our relationship - past St. Wayne's boatshed. . .

SAM. Michael, don't ... (he's really getting to her)

TAMSIN. We've got a backyard psychiatrist on board.

But MICHAEL isn't going to be distracted by TAMSIN. He's moving in for the kill.

MICHAEL. All those years ago ... when it stopped drizzling, and the rainbow came out. I held your hand in mine (taking her hand)...

SAM. With half the first 8 looking on. (then another thought) Where did it all go, Michael?

MICHAEL. You got it in court this morning, dear.

NIGEL, furious, is making a very loud and clumsy effort to shove the audio cassette into the boat's PA system. He flings a disgusted look back at them, groaning at the sheer awfulness of it all. As the MUSIC starts:

MICHAEL. May I have one last dance?

Much to NIGEL's horror MICHAEL scoops SAMANTHA into his arms and they start dancing cheek to cheek around the boat. Something schmaltzy like the Reel's *"This guy's in love"* underscores MICHAEL and SAMANTHA's cosy duet.

NIGEL just stares at them open mouthed. Then he starts following them. Closely.

SAMANTHA, ignoring NIGEL, encourages other people to join in the dance. Like a kind of bridal waltz, gathering more guests in as it goes along.

The more she dances the more flamboyant and happy and extrovert SAMANTHA becomes. She laughs outright at some sweet nothing MICHAEL has just whispered in her ear.

In despair NIGEL turns to TAMSIN. She's deposited herself stiffly in a chair. Refusing obviously, to have anything to do with the waltz, whether bridal or otherwise.

NIGEL. Can't you do something about this?

TAMSIN. Darling, I'm washing my hands of the whole sordid business.

By now another dance song has come on the party tape - something from *Ice House*

MICHAEL sings along with the chorus, with SAM gazing adoringly into his eyes.

MICHAEL. Hey, little girl,

Where will you go?

Who will you run to now?

MICHAEL and SAMANTHA swan past NIGEL and TAMSIN, quite close. NIGEL just glares at them, with bleak distaste. He follows after them, forlornly trying to stand between them. Almost trying to dance a threesome.

SAM. Nigel, please...

In disgust, NIGEL turns to one of the guests and invites her to dance with him.

NIGEL. May I?

Surprisingly the GUEST agrees and for a few moments NIGEL tries to take his mind off SAM and MICHAEL getting all very cosy together.

But even this doesn't work so he breaks off dancing with the guest and turns to tap MICHAEL on the shoulder.

No response. So NIGEL taps again.

MICHAEL. Look, push off will you, Neville.

NIGEL taps a third time, MICHAEL simply shrugs NIGEL's hand off his shoulder.

MICHAEL If you want to dance, why don' t you ask your doctor? I'm sure she'd be thrilled.

TAMSIN. No she wouldn't.

NIGEL. (to MICHAEL) She wouldn't.

LURLENE. I would.

LURLENE starts gyrating awkwardly around NIGEL. He sullenly joins in. But is just barely moving.

In any case LURLENE is clearly a-rhythmical. The effect of the two of them trying to dance is really quite bizarre.

Eventually NIGEL can stand it no longer.

He breaks off with LURLENE and wanders back to the loving couple. They look at him, hesitating a moment.

NIGEL. (bluntly) Can I get you a drink ? (more to SAM)

MICHAEL. Only if you get someone to taste it for poison first.

Both MICHAEL and SAMANTHA break up at this witticism. Finding it a huge joke.

Which only serves to send NIGEL's blood pressure soaring. He barely contains his anger and walks stiffly down to the table with the cake on it where he takes the large carving knife (with a pretty pink ribbon tied to it) and strides menacingly back up towards MICHAEL who has

his back turned to him.

NIGEL holds the knife up and appears to be about to plunge it several inches into the back of MICHAEL's neck. At which point SAM, facing NIGEL, looks up in horror.

SAM. Nigel!

Registering her fright, MICHAEL swings around, so that NIGEL quickly drops the threatening posture, lowering the knife to an innocuous level.

NIGEL. (to SAMANTHA) I think we should cut the cake now.

SAM. (exasperated sigh, peeved) Oh, if you insist, NIGEL.

NIGEL. It was your idea remember.

SAMANTHA huffily takes the knife while NIGEL hands his Instamatic camera over to MRS FOWLER.

NIGEL. Would you mind, ah...

LURLENE. Oh sure, love, By jeeze you two must be very, very happy.

Their grim expressions belie the fact. And so with barely concealed distaste they both take the knife and hold it over a smaller (real) cake - other than the one SAMANTHA came out of.

MRS. FOWLER lines up the shot, not displaying a great deal of skill with the camera. She studies the buttons and viewfinder vaguely.

MRS. FOWLER. Ah…

So NIGEL comes back to help her out.

NIGEL Look through there and just-press this button.

LURLENE. Right you are.

NIGEL resumes his place next to SAMANTHA holding the knife together.

LURLENE. Say cheese.

The most painful of wooden smiles spreads across the faces of the defacto lovers.

SAM. English stilton.

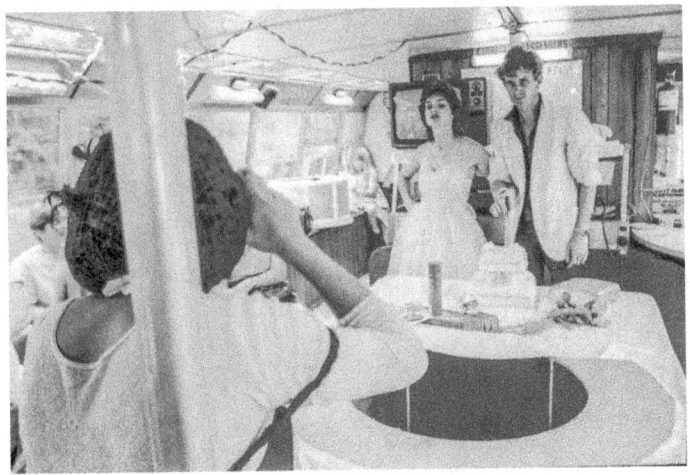

MRS. FOWLER hits the button and the flash goes off. There's polite applause as they cut the cake together, getting it sort of mashed up. MICHAEL leads the response enjoying their obvious discomfort enormously. SAMANTHA pulls away from NIGEL and glances out through a window.

SAM. Oh look we're docking at the Como landing. And there's mummy's butler, Kurt! How wonderful, he's brought refreshments and everything. I must go and see if she's home. Michael darling, could you find my wrap?

There's the sound of a 'gong' and the title:

"INTERMISSION"

…comes on the video as the boat nudges into the Como park jetty.

INTERMISSION

Further fuelling NIGEL's brooding jealousy, MICHAEL and SAMANTHA slip off the boat early…

And make their not-so-covert way up towards Mummy's Toorak mansion.

Meanwhile, MUSIC comes on over the boat's PA As the rest of SAMANTHA's guests move out of the boat up onto the Como jetty where KURT, in his butler's uniform, servepeople coffee and orange juice, wedding/divorce cake and biscuits. For a while MRS. FOWLER gives him a hand but later seems more intent on finding a shore-based toilet.

NIGEL comes out expressing his frustration to TAMSIN. She's urging him to just "cool it".

So NIGEL mingles uncomfortably with some of the guests, clearly agitated at SAMANTHA's continued absence. He wanders up to various groups and bleakly asks if they've seen his lover or her ex husband?

After ten minutes of repeated inquiries to a negative response, NIGEL's anxiety builds to something approaching blind panic and he finally hurtles on up the path towards Mummies' mansion threatening to aid the collapse of MICHAEL's face in on itself. In fact he fully intends to "spread that upper class moustache all over the worm's dial"… before disappearing into the night.

After another ten minutes or so MICHAEL and SAMANTHA wander back down the path clearly unscathed by NIGEL's previous threats. Who remains missing. They chat amiably with various guests hanging there under the coloured lights and share straws over a single orange juice. They recall some of the lighter moments of their married life together, and really carry on to all intents and purposes as if they'd just been re-engaged.

Eventually SAMANTHA notices the hour and reminds KURT that it's time for mummy's foot massage. She goes back to her guests and says anyway (somewhat conspiratorially) that while NIGEL's not around she wants to show them all one of the ads he did for the Balwyn Chamber of commerce. NIGEL doesn't want to admit that he's made an ad. It's such an embarrassment to a wannabe *auteur*, but SAMANTHA thinks the ad is quite amusing and-suggests if they make their way back on board *The Yarra Princess* while KURT cleans up, she'll put it on quickly before NIGEL can stop her.

So people make their way back onto the boat:

SECOND ACT

(Downstream Journey)

Back on board the *Yarra Princess* SAMANTHA puts Nigel's "commercial" video on.

Over shots of NIGEL appearing under a series of signs indicating that he's in the Balwyn shopping centre there's a chorus of voices singing:

CHORUS. (on screen) "Hey girls that's Balwyn callin'

Hey girls that's Balwyn callin'

Yes girls that's Balwyn callin' ' . . .

NIGEL. (on screen) Hi, I'm Nigel Davidson, Nigel Davidson film productions— I was wondering if you could tell me why Balwyn is the most exciting place in Melbourne to shop?

He's pointing the microphone at two girls in the street who sort of look blank.

GIRL. (on screen) I dunno.

NIGEL stops a punk looking character in dark glasses.

PUNK. (on screen) It's not, it's not! You've got it all wrong.

The next interviewee is a kindly faced, well rounded, middle-aged man.

MIDDLE-AGED MAN. (on screen) Well, ah...(obviously can't think of any reason)

NIGEL strides after various OLDER WOMEN who keep walking, eyes straight ahead refusing even to acknowledge him.

NIGEL. (on screen) I was wondering if you could tell me...ah ...(he's panting, trying to keep up) excuse me I was ... I'm Nigel Davidson and I was wondering if . . .

The OLDER WOMEN keep walking.

NIGEL has found ANOTHER MIDDLE AGED MAN with a YOUNG BOY and he's only too happy to talk.

DES FLETCHER. (on screen) Great to meet you Nigel, my name's Desmond Fletcher

of the Red Cross.

NIGEL. (on screen) How are you.

DES FLETCHER. (on screen) I'm good. This is my son James...

NIGEL bows down, half smiling to the YOUNG BOY

NIGEL. (on screen) Hullo, how do you do..

DES FLETCHER. (on screen) My younger son, James. My other son's not here - George.

NIGEL. (on screen) How old's he?

DES FLETCHER. (on screen) James is 10, George is 13.

Next NIGEL has bailed up a MAN IN HIS THIRTIES who leans back, almost defensively against a butcher shop wall. NIGEL reacts, conscious of the camera, doesn't want to look like a stalker.

MAN IN HIS THIRTIES. (on screen) Oh, fantastic place to shop - if that's what you want me to say.

NIGEL. (on screen) Oh, no...I want you to be perfectly honest.

MAN IN HIS THIRTIES. (on screen) Oh. No. Well I think it's one of the better ones around. I think so yes, compared to other suburbs.

=

Back to DES FLETCHER.

DES FLETCHER. (on screen) To shop? Now that's interesting. I wouldn't say it's the most *interesting* place to shop. The thing I like about it is that since I live here I know most...

NIGEL nods politely, going along with the flow, but wondering when the hell DES is going to shut-up!

DES FLETCHER. (on screen cont.)... of the shopkeepers, they're a very friendly lot of people. I can get almost everything I want. Not everything. But almost everything ...

NIGEL now has stopped an ELDERLY COUPLE. He in his pork pie straw hat, she is holding the shopping basket.

ELDERLY LADY. (on screen) Oh it's a terrific shopping centre.

ELDERLY MAN. (on screen) With such a huge variety here.

Just what NIGEL wants to hear.

NIGEL. (on screen) Oh great.

ELDERLY MAN. (on screen) The prices are right, too.

NIGEL. (on screen) The prices are right in Balwyn.

ELDERLY LADY. (on screen) Yes in all the shops.

    NIGEL beams at them.

NIGEL. (on screen) Ok, thank you very much. That's wonderful. . .

    ELDERLY COUPLE walk off and NIGEL looks so happy he's lost for words.

NIGEL. (on screen) That's really wonderful, that's just. . .

    He looks at the camera a moment.

NIGEL. (on screen thinks) I don't think we can use it.

    Back with DES, NIGEL is still nodding politely wondering how the hell to turn this man off.

    NIGEL looks at the camera, imitating the wind-up signal he's getting from the cameraman.

DES FLETCHER. (on screen - reeling them off on his fingers) If I want a suit I go into the city, if I want my wife's scent I go down to Camberwell. But I can get practically everything I want in the Balwyn shopping centre.

NIGEL. (on screen seizing an opportunity to butt in) Right, practically everything you want in Balwyn. Thank you very much.

DES FLETCHER. (on screen) Nice meeting you anyway.

NIGEL. (on screen) Yeah.

Next we're on a middle aged woman.

A MIDDLE AGED WOMAN (on screen) I don't know-- you better ask my daughter

NIGEL. (on screen turning to her) well?

DAUGHTER. (on screen) It's close to home.

NIGEL. (on screen) It's close to home.

DAUGHTER. (on screen) Ah - I dunno.

(on screen they all LAUGH)

Now NIGEL has bailed up A GARAGE MECHANIC in his overalls.

A GARAGE MECHANIC. (on screen) I don't think it is the most exciting place to shop.

NIGEL. (on screen grimly) Thank you very much.

And THE MECHANIC walks off. NIGEL follows, looking as if he could thump the man.

Cut to ANOTHER MAN fronting the camera.

NIGEL. (on screen having trouble remembering the question) Ahm what is. . . what the ah. . . ah what, what I am. . .am I what am I asking?

NIGEL turns to the camera with a puzzled look.

VOICE OFF. (on screen behind the camera) Why is Balwyn the most...

NIGEL. (on screen gets it) Why is Balwyn the most exciting place to shop?

Finally NIGEL leans down to talk confidentially with a couple of poodles tied up outside the health food shop.

NIGEL holds the mike out for them to bark into. but the dogs just back away.

NIGEL. (on screen to dogs) Ahm, I'm doing a survey for the Balwyn Chamber of Commerce about shopping in Balwyn and I was wondering if you could tell me what do you think of Balwyn as one of the most exciting places in Melbourne to shop?

NIGEL holds the mike out for them to bark into. But the dogs just back away.

Back to the kindly faced, well rounded middle aged man from tale beginning who could'nt make up his mind.

MIDDLE-AGED MAN. (on screen) Anything else?

NIGEL. (on screen) No - that's all, thank you very much.

Again, over various shots of NIGEL in the Balwyn shopping centre, pointing at various signs etc. we hear the theme song:

CHORUS. (on screen) "Hey girls that's Balwyn callin'
    Hey girls that's Balwyn callin'
    Yes girls that's Balwyn callin' ' . . .

MICHAEL has come back onto the boat and immediately switches the video off.

MICHAEL. God, wasn't that appalling? (calling out) Hey, Neville, it's Balwyn calling!

He yells it out the doorway, since NIGEL still hasn't re-appeared, although everybody else, (except LURLENE) is back on board.

MICHAEL turns back inside the boat laughing.

MICHAEL. Here comes the great streak.

NIGEL is racing down the path towards the jetty, there's murder in his look as he leaps back onto the boat. MICHAEL gives him a slow hand clap.

MICHAEL. Oh, very good Neville.

NIGEL is absolutely furious. Rounding on SAMANTHA.

NIGEL. Did you show him the Balwyn film?

SAMANTHA. They all loved it, darling.

NIGEL. You're laughing at -me, aren't you?

MICHAEL. No - just your film.

NIGEL. Come on pal, put ya dukes up.

NIGEL shapes up to thump MICHAEL, MICHAEL dips his fingers in the punch and flicks them at NIGEL, spraying him.

MICHAEL. Just cool down, Neville.

NIGEL. (dancing around MICHAEL) Come on, put 'em up.

MICHAEL is backing away towards the rear of the boat, he draws an imaginary line between them with his shoe.

MICHAEL. Neville ! Don't step over that line.

This stops NIGEL, he hesitates, looks down at the floor, then lifting his foot in quite an exaggerated manner he deliberately steps over it.

NIGEL. (challenging) MICHAEL! (so there!)

SAMANTHA. (excited) Oh he did it!

TAMSIN becomes a little concerned, any rational restraint has obviously snapped in NIGEL. MICHAEL has goaded him close to the brink.

TAMSIN. Nigel, there are other ways of expressing your anger.

MICHAEL ducks behind TAMSIN, and ever valiant, uses her as a shield.

NIGEL swings out a couple of times, and MICHAEL dances TAMSIN around

in front of him, ducking and weaving. But eventually, inevitably, a punch of NIGEL's goes astray and smacks TAMSIN square on the jaw. She drops to the floor like a log.

NIGEL hangs there, horrified.

NIGEL. You made me hit my therapist!

Now NIGEL loses it completely. He leaps over the stricken TAMSIN and goes straight for the jugular, they wrestle clumsily around the boat for a bit, until finally MICHAEL has NIGEL around the neck, and is squeezing the life out of him.

SAM. (sweetly) Oh, you're not . . . fighting over me are you? (quietly chuffed)

NIGEL. (gasping) Stop. . . looking. . . so . . . thrilled. . . by. . . the. . . idea.

MICHAEL. You stole my wife from me you pseudo human.

NIGEL. Can't we sit down and discuss this?

There's a sharp crack. NIGEL goes limp and falls back to the ground.

SAM. (sudden alarm) What was that?

TAMSIN. (from her own prone position of the floor) Sounded like a couple of vertebrae snapping.

SAM. You've broken his neck!

TAMSIN sits bolt upright. Comes back to her feet.

MICHAEL. (looking rather pleased with himself) Yes. Damn pity really, couple more ads like that and they might have banned commercials from television altogether.

TAMSIN is bending over NIGEL.

SAM. I've never seen a dead body before. It's disgusting. What are we going to do?

MICHAEL. (after a quick thought) Weighing up the pros and cons, I'd say: chuck him overboard.

TAMSIN.   )
         -- (together) What?
SAM.   )

MICHAEL. We'll deep six the bastard, let the sharks have a go.

SAM. Oh - poor NIGEL.

    Suddenly there's a blue flashing light on the jetty', the sound of A SIREN, and someone clearing their throat through A MEGAPHONE.

LANCE. (voice off through a megaphone) Hold fast *Yarra Princess* this is the police speaking.

SAM. (brightly) Yarra Princess ? Oh, is someone calling me?

TAMSIN. (looking out) It's the police.

LANCE. (off) Do not attempt to leave the wharf as we are coming aboard, over.

MICHAEL quickly checks through a window, the siren is coming back on and the blue flashing light approaching through the darkness. He sticks his hand exaggeratedly, menacingly into his coat pocket and points it around at the boat generally.

MICHAEL. (going over to splash gin from the punch table all over NIGEL)

He slipped and fell, right? (thinking fast) he. . . he . . . he'd been drinking since ten this morning and there was nothing we could do.

SAM. (panicked) They'll never believe a story like that, Michael.

TAMSIN. If the papers get hold of this, your name will be mud in East Malvern.

But that's the least of MICHAEL's worries right now.

LANCE.(voice off, puffing through the megaphone as he runs towards the boat) This is senior sergeant Lance Tippler speaking, heave to skipper we're coming aboard, over.

SAMANTHA starts to become hysterical.

MICHAEL suddenly produces a small Belgian pistol from his pocket.

SAM. Never! Never believe it!

MICHAEL points the weapon directly at her.

MICHAEL. They will if you tell them.

TAMSIN takes a deep breath.

TAMSIN. This is absolutely preposterous.

The approaching SIREN grows louder. Out on the jetty two police officers rapidly approach, pushing people aside.

Back on board MICHAEL becomes desperate.

MICHAEL. Get him under the table.

SAM. What?

MICHAEL. Move the bloody table, we'll hide him under that.

SAM. I can't lift it, Michael, it's too heavy.

MICHAEL. God! It's like going camping with you Samantha. Skipper, give her a hand.

So JIM comes over and somehow the three of them (TAMSIN SAMANTHA and JIM)

manage to bundle NIGEL out of sight under the table to which the large mock "wedding cake" is attached.

SAMANTHA Makes a quick prayer, blesses herself.

SAM. For what we're about to receive may the lord make us truely thankful.

TASMIN. Forcrissake, amen.

MICHAEL points the gun around the boat, including everybody.

MICHAEL. Right, I'll slaughter the first person that speaks.

He quickly hides the gun as the boat starts moving and LANCE and CONST. CATHY WATERMAN leap aboard... CATHY wears a police constable's uniform, jodhpurs and boots. A sophisticated accounting computer and tax forms hang from her belt. She also carries a briefcase wrapped in a plastic bag. LANCE wears a trench coat, mutton chops, inflatable floatation device, swimming goggles on top of a bowler hat and two long tubes of shark repellent dangling from his belt inside the trench coat. He stumbles awkwardly down the steps from the front door.

CATHY. Right, everybody freeze! This is a tax raid.

LANCE (putting the megaphone back up to his lips) Kindly have your chequebooks and wallets open ready for inspection, thank you!

CATHY. We want all financial documents in mint condition.

LANCE. (eyeing the audience narrowly as he moves up "his" side of the boat) So don't try any scribbled out amounts, or missing pages, or altered balance sheets, thank you very much.

TAMSIN. Oh look, it's Mr. Plod and Noddy.

LANCE glares at her, takes the briefcase and flings it down in front of the "GUESTS".

The briefcase is contained within a large clear plastic bag which is sealed at the top with a tag reading "Exhibit A".

LANCE. This briefcase was found dragging along the bottom of the river behind your boat.

CATHY. (eyeing off her side of the boat) Somebody here is in a great deal of trouble.

Despite MICHAEL's close watch on her, SAMANTHA steps brightly forward.

LANCE is stowing away his effluent resistor mask.

SAM. Oh, surely there must be some mistake.

CATHY. No mistake, madam. I am Constable Cathy Waterman, of the Melbourne Mounted-Acquatic Police. North side.

LANCE. And I am Senior Sergeant Lance Tippler, Vice Gaming and Other Expenses squad. South side.

TAMSIN. Vice, Gaming, and Other Expenses? Don't you mean "Offences" Sergeant?

LANCE. What you call "expenses."

CATHY. To us they're "offences."

LANCE. From your tax evasion. . .

CATHY. We feel aversion.

LANCE. (singing) Expenses.

CATHY. Offenses.

LANCE. Evasion

CATHY. Aversion

SAM. (trilling along with them) Let's call the whole thing off. . .

LANCE. (breaking out of the song) Are you kidding?

> TAMSIN, throws a quick glance at MICHAEL who is still fading into in
>
> background. His hand is firmly planted in his pocket, but TAMSIN decides to risk it. She takes a deep breath and. . .

TAMSIN. Sergeant -

LANCE rounds on her menacingly.

LANCE. Your income for the last 12 months, madam?

TAMSIN is caught off guard.

TAMSIN. Well about seven... eight...

CATHY. Quickly, quickly.

TAMSIN. Seventy ... eight ... thousand dollars.

LANCE and CATHY chuckle derisively. They clearly don't believe her.

CATHY. (taking a form from around her belt, holding it up) I trust then, you're familiar with the tax form "Investment and Property Income?

TAMSIN. Yes, yes, I should think so.

LANCE. (pointing at it as CATHY opens the page) You'd consequently be aware of the "other expenses" column?

TAMSIN. (nods) Mmmm (unsure of what will happen next).

CATHY. Well, that's us. The "Other Expenses Squad".

Suddenly there's a panicked yell from the jetty as the Yarra Princess pulls away.

LURLENE. (off) Hey, wait for me!

Everybody spins around to see LURLENE left behind on the jetty, with KURT there about to restrain her from an obvious tendency to jump in and make a swim for it - after the boat.

CATHY. Just a minute, sir.

LANCE. Wha...What is it? (can't understand all the fuss).

LURLENE is jumping up and down on the jetty, yelling, waving at them to come back,

LURLENE. You could've have waited! I had to find a toilet!

Already, however, the YARRA PRINCESS is 50-100 metres away.

CATHY. There appears to be an odd looking woman, dressed in a white apron and...black tutu, sir.

LANCE. God it's amazing what some people will get up to on drugs these days isn't it?

CATHY. Looks like she's trying to jump in!

LANCE. (wearily) You'd better warn her, constable.

So CATHY takes the megaphone and speaks through the front door.

CATHY. (amplified) I'm afraid you've missed the boat, madam, stand back from the wharf, we don't want a drowning and toxic poisoning on our hands.

LANCE. Does she look like a tax risk, constable?

CATHY. I hardly think so, sir. Not on her income.

LANCE. Oh very well, notify the poisons squad. Have them send their white ambulance around. We can't waste any more time on it.

>   As CATHY calls up the poison's squad on her pocket radio MICHAEL turns to a nearby-audience member:

MICHAEL. You just can't get good help these days can you?

>   LANCE pulls a whistle out, gives a couple of SHARP BLASTS to quieten the boat.

LANCE. Right, bit of focus thank you. We're not going on with this until we have your complete attention.

TAMSIN. Actually, it's rather fortunate you've arrived, Senior Sergeant

because there's somebody amongst us who's got a g...g...(gun).

MICHAEL jabs the snout of his pistol into her back through the lining of his coat.

TAMSIN. (cont.) ... a... g - reat big undisclosed tax liability.

CATHY and LANCE chuckle derisively.

LANCE. Oh we know that...

CATHY. That's why we're here.

CATHY and LANCE stride up and down on their separate sides of the boat, keeping in step, imitating each other's gestures.

CATHY. Some months ago while riding mounted patrol along Batman avenue I happened to notice strange goings on aboard certain Yarra rivercraft. Parties and suspicious general revelry.

LANCE. Naturally, I seconded Constable Waterman to my Department from the Mounted Acquatic Squad, and I'm pleased to say *my* efforts . . .

CATHY clears her throat, anticipating praise.

LANCE. . . and *her* efforts have paid off handsomely.

CATHY. Thank you Sergeant.

LANCE. And thank you constable. Oh yes, I'm quite sure (corrects himself) *we're* quite sure, I've - we've - netted here one of the biggest tax cheats and financial charlatans in the whole evasion industry.

SAM.(singing it) Bingo!

TAMSIN rushes forward, away from MICHAEL.

TAMSIN. Sergeant, I think you're missing the main *body* (pointing back towards the table) of evidence to table (trying to draw his attention down the back where Nigel's "body" lies hidden).

MICHAEL rushes after TAMSIN in order to contain her, he places his arm firmly around her. Affectionate, but restraining.

MICHAEL. This is nothing more than a harmless party, Sergeant.

SAM. Yes, to celebrate my liberation.

LANCE. Don't tell me liberation's harmless! What with tax loopholes you could drive a leopard tank through! The whole thing's out of control I tell you.

SAM. I don't see any evidence of that.

LANCE. No evidence, eh?

LANCE swings around clicks his fingers at CATHY.

LANCE. Would you estimate the net income of the assembled company, constable.

CATHY. Including interlocking trusts and covert directorships?

LANCE. Of course.

LANCE and CATHY move to the front of the boat
and stand on either side of the skipper. CATHY takes
her mini-computer out.

CATHY. Right, could I have a show of hands of all those who live on the north side of the river?

She starts counting as a few nervous hands go up.

CATHY. (counting)... three, four, six, ten... eleven low income earners, sir.

MICHAEL. (to someone nearby) So that's what they look like.

LANCE pounds his fist into an open palm, there's
obviously little joy in low income earners for him.

LANCE. Damn!

CATHY. Now hands up all those who live on the south side of the river..

A few more hands go up, some a little uncertainty.

LANCE. Come on, come on...

CATHY is counting.

CATHY. Twenty eight, thirty, thirty four richies, sir.

LANCE is apoplectic, he zeroes in on some poor unfortunate "guest".

LANCE. You didn't put your hand up either time! Are you telling me you live in the middle of the river or something?!

He comes back to stand next to CATHY, composes himself a little, drying the sweat off the inside rim of his hat. While CATHY makes a few calculations on her computer:

CATHY. Right, a show of hands of all those who drive a European car?

A few hands go up, including SAMANTHA and MICHAEL.

LANCE. Come on, come on, we'll find out eventually.

SAM. (aside to MICHAEL) I got the BMW remember.

CATHY. (quickly) Right, now keep it up if it's not a Volkswagon.

SAMANTHA's hand stays up while CATHY enters these figures into the computer.

LANCE. (skeptically) I suppose the rest of you ride bicycles to the stock exchange ?

A couple of sheepish hands go up.

LANCE. And two bicycles, constable.

CATHY. Right, Senior. Now, hands up all those people with access to a private tennis court.

As a few people admit it:

LANCE. (rubbing his hands gleefully) Ah ha! I find that very hard to believe. (the-low number).

CATHY moves over to one of them. All friendly suddenly.

CATHY. Oh really? Could I pop over next weekend, my backhand's

been really off lately and I've had terrible trouble with my serve.   . .actually, we're not a bad mixed double, you know...

From up the front of the boat where he has now positioned himself LANCE looks daggers at her, pointing to his watch.

LANCE. Constable? Time is money, son.

CATHY straightens, comes straight back to the front of the boat making a few final calculations.

CATHY. Right, estimated net income of all the people on this boat-- approximately thirty four million eight hundred and ninety thousand, four hundred and fifty three dollars and 25 cents, dollars, sir! (saluting him)

LANCE. (savouring the moment, rubbing his hands in anticipation) And total tax paid by these people on that income?

CATHY. (another quick calculation) Exactly. . .a dollar ninety eight.

LANCE gives a WHOOP of joy.

LANCE. We've done it, Constable! This is bigger than the Springvale Buffalo's gambling night.

CATHY. You were right, sir, you'd said you'd find them on the luxury party circuit.

LANCE. (eyeing them derisively) Like flies round the compost heap, constable.

    Again TAMSIN comes forward, unable to contain herself.

TAMSIN. But surely Sergeant, your argument lacks *body* (pointing back under the table).

    LANCE takes out a biro and clicks it stylishly, about to write-in his official notebook. The impertinence of questioning his methodology.

LANCE. Your name, madam?

TAMSIN. Dr. Tamsin Smythe. Dip. Psyche, Oxon and Bar, Dip. Thong University. I am one of *the* Smythes of East Camberwell, we happen to be a highly distinguished medical family. In fact all my relatives were in institutions. My grandfather was a high court judge.

LANCE. Oh yes, and I'm the king of Nyasaland. (indicating CATHY) I'd like you to meet the Duchess of Sumatra.

    CATHY and LANCE break up at this. Enjoying the moment.

CATHY. (chuckling) You're a real knee slapper Sergeant.

LANCE. Yes. (then quickly sobering) Check her out for oh.... (looking TAMSIN up and down) credit cards, all access accounts, overdraft limits, debenture shares, franked dividends and partnership securities.

CATHY. What about fraudulent Medibank refunds, sir?

Damn. LANCE wishes he'd thought of that.

LANCE. Clever, clever... (tapping his nose).

CATHY indicates TAMSIN's briefcase.

CATHY. If you wouldn't mind opening your briefcase please, doctor.

TAMSIN. What?

CATHY. Your briefcase.

TAMSIN. (clutching her precious briefcase) This case contains private in confidence material between a doctor and her patients.

CATHY gives an impatient sigh. Indicates for TAMSIN to hand it over.

TAMSIN. I wish to speak to my lawyer.

LANCE comes forward and gently takes the
briefcase, opening it.

LANCE. (glancing into it) Oh yes, yes sure, doc. We'd all
like to speak to our lawyers...wouldn't we? 'Trouble is, you
see, they hardly ever want to talk to us.

Without taking his eyes off TAMSIN, LANCE tips
the contents onto the floor. We see various books
about body posture, esoteric healing, mental illness
and Mills and Boon novels tumbling out.

Suddenly NIGEL's BLEEPER goes off under the
table.

LANCE and CATHY freeze.

LANCE. What was that? (the bleeper stops)

CATHY. Sounded like a bleeper, sir.

LANCE. Is there somebody here enjoying themselves when they should be at work- hmmm? Well?

He waits. No one moves.

LANCE. There's a phone over there, (pointing to one near 'JIM' on the boat's elaborate dashboard) Go and ring your office. Go on.

Nobody moves.

CATHY. Perhaps they're planning to claim the party as an entertainment expense, Senior.

LANCE. Is there no end to the infamy? What a pretty bunch, eh? (a sweeping glare around the audience) Take a good look, Constable there's the face of crime out there, staring back at us, looking as if butter wouldn't melt in its mouth, all sweet and plummy, a nation of thieves I tell you!

CATHY. (cutting in, impatient) Oh get on with it.

LANCE swings around her, stunned.

LANCE. What?

SAMANTHA decides to rescue the situation.

SAM. Inspector, could I have a wee word in your ear?

LANCE. A what in my ear, madam?

TAMSIN. (putting her scattered belongings back into her briefcase) A wee.

SAM. How absolutely fab it is that you've arrived... I was only saying to my husband, (putting an arm through MICHAEL's)

SAM. Ah... (he jabs her in the back with the gun still hidden in his coat pocket)

MICHAEL. Sydney (nodding, smiling at LANCE).

SAM. (unsure now) Sydney, er...

MICHAEL. Lumley.

SAM. S ... Sydney Lumley, that wasn't it about time ... we ah, (checks with MICHAEL, he's nodding) that we ah, (rummages through her purse) subscribed for some tickets to the ah...Policeman's Ball.

MICHAEL. (butting in) White light disco.

SAMANTHA nods, smiles, thrusts a thick wad of Indonesian rupees into LANCE's hand. He looks dumbfounded. Letting the cash just lie there in his open palm. MICHAEL rolls his eyes, looks to heaven.

SAM. After all we do... do a lot of charity work Mi-my-Sydney and I, Mi... my husband, Sydney...

She smiles brightly.

SAM. ...Lumley...

MICHAEL grimaces, LANCE looks slowly from the thick wad of notes back up to SAMANTHA.

LANCE. (hoarse whisper, thick with emotion) Your name madam?

SAM. Samantha Har... (she stops, realizes she's about to blow it)

MICHAEL. (prompts) Lumley.

SAM. Hart-Lumley

LANCE. Are you aware, Mrs. Hart-Lumley, that you've just caused to be passed into my possession (holds them up for CATHY to calculate by weight) the equivalent of...

CATHY. (holding the notes, moving them up and down) $2,785 dollars.

LANCE. (looking at them) In... Indonesian rupiah?

SAM. Well as NIGEL says...

TAMSIN. (quickly) Said. Nigel said (emphasising the past tense)

SAM. Said - We'll all be Indonesian one day.

LANCE. Not if I can stop you lot from white-anting our Aussie economy.

CATHY. Who's Nigel?

SAM. (too quickly, casually) Oh just a friend.

TAMSIN. Ex-friend. (looking uncertainly from MICHAEL back to CATHY again)

MICHAEL glares at her

LANCE. (holding the money up) Are you attempting to bribe an officer of the law, madam?

SAM hesitates

CATHY. Well, madam?

SAM. (throwing up her hands) Oh forheavensake! It's just some loose change. I had to fly rather quickly back from Denpasar this morning.

CATHY snatches the money off LANCE and hands it back to SAMANTHA.

CATHY. (firmly) We are not bribable.

LANCE looks actually a little disappointed.

SAM. But it's only a donation.

LANCE quickly retrieves the money from SAM and pockets it.

LANCE. Well, that's different.

CATHY looks shocked, but LANCE launches straight on.

LANCE. Could I trouble you to open your bag, madam.

SAM. (appalled) What? in public?

CATHY. That is going a bit far, sergeant.

In a sudden frenzy LANCE snatches SAM's purse and carries it away towards the front of the boat opening it and looking inside

LANCE. Don't tell me tax evaders have got rights!

Then, with his back turned and hunched over SAM's purse LANCE deliberately and quite clumsily shakes a savings account passbook into the bag from inside his coat sleeve. Then turns around for all to see and makes a big point of extracting the passbook.

LANCE. Hullo, hullo what's this? (holding it up)

A savings account! (as if he's struck gold)

TAMSIN. You put that there!

There's a GENERAL MURMUR of agreement.

LANCE. (taken aback) What?

SAM. You deliberately planted that on me!

LANCE. (like child, caught red handed) No I didn't.

SAM.   )
       -- (together) Yes you did.
TAMSIN.   )

TAMSIN. Why the whole boat saw you. (turning around to them) Didn't we?

Again everybody nods and agrees with her.

ALL. Yairs...

LANCE slowly rounds on them.

LANCE. Oh- I get it (spits it out) It's the old "you-planted-it-on-me" routine is it? Besmirch the poor copper's good name. My god you crooks! The depths to which you'll sink. You see now Constable the true meaning of the term "bottom of the harbour"! Down there with the crabs and car bodies. It's disgusting

CATHY. Yes, senior.

SAMANTHA's certainly not taking this from a worm like LANCE.

SAM. I've never been so insulted in all my life!

LANCE. Did anybody here see me plant anything at all upon this suspect's person?

MICHAEL)   No.

　　---(together)

ALL)   Yes.

LANCE looks like he's about to thump them, he pounds his fist into his palm instead, only MICHAEL seems to be playing along. So LANCE turns to him.

LANCE. Why would anybody want to dump a book with ... (holding it out for CATHY calculate).

CATHY. (Takes it, reads) $743,000...

LANCE. ... in it (eyeballing MICHAEL) Well, sir? Could you hazard a guess?

MICHAEL. It's got nothing to do with me Sergeant, I'm afraid I'm no longer married to the woman. I suspect she hid it from my solicitors in the Family Court last week.

SAM. Michael!

MICHAEL. (correcting) Sydney.

LANCE. Very likely, sir, very likely, we're dealing with a peculiarly greedy animal in your average defrauder of the public purse.

SAM. (appalled) This is an outrage I tell you.

CATHY. No - sorry (reading the cover) It's a Zodiac Savers Account.

LANCE. Bank?

CATHY. (opening the first page) The "Loan Arranger and Deep Sea File Cash Management Trust of lower Port Moresby".

LANCE. (conceding) Well, I must say it does gladden the heart to see a woman of your means investing in a third world country.

SAM. Yes. (she doesn't care now, she feels betrayed by MICHAEL) My former husband had a fabulously successful Bird of Paradise export trade there.

LANCE and CATHY look slowly from SAM back to
MICHAEL.

LANCE. Birds of Paradise can't be exported from New Guinea, madam, they're a highly protected and endangered species.

CATHY. There's a 20 year jail sentence attendant upon that.

Both look back to SAMANTHA. Behind them MICHAEL points the gun directly at her. SAM's eyes widen.

SAM. (flummoxed) Oh ah, well yes, I think perhaps it was a...

MICHAEL. (whispers) Shut-up!

SAM. Goldmine.

MICHAEL. No!

SAM. No -

LANCE and CATHY look from one to the other, as soon as their eyes are off MICHAEL he points the gun back at SAMANTHA.

MICHAEL. It was a plantation.

Obviously making it up as they go along.

SAM. And all the natives...

MICHAEL. . . suddenly went bush to fight a tribal war. . .

SAM. So the (checking with him) the. . . harvest failed...

MICHAEL.)   and we all lost a great deal of coffee

    ---(together)

SAM.   )   and we all lost a' great deal of gold (correcting) coffee.

MICHAEL. (at SAM) No!

CATHY. Remarkable.

LANCE. (chuckles) Sounds like somebody spilt *the beans* to me. Dropped a *little nugget* of vital evidence. (enjoying his clever word play)

CATHY. Well which is it, madam, gold or coffee?

SAM. Look - that book, it's - an utter fabrication.

CATHY. (checking inside again) The book does appear to belong to a certain Samantha Hart-Lumley, sir.

LANCE. And you claim you're *not* the said woman madam?

SAM. Which woman?

CATHY. Samantha Hart-Lumley!

SAM. Did I say that?

CATHY. Yes.

LANCE. Yes.

MICHAEL. Yes.

TAMSIN. Yes.

LANCE. (holding the bank book out towards her) Yet you don't wish to retain the $743,000?

SAM. (realising) Oh is that mine? I've never been known to refuse money in my life.

She goes to reach for it, LANCE holds it back.

CATHY. We'll need a sample of your signature.

SAM. Oh but I don't have any paper on me...(looking around)

   LANCE places a withdrawal slip on top of the book and hands it over to her.

LANCE. Ahm, just ah. . . in the rectangle there (indicating).

   SAM goes to sign, crosses out the first attempt, ("Hart-Byrne")

SAM. Oh...

   Then writes "Samantha Hart-Lumley"

   LANCE immediately whips book and slip away.

SAM. (a little curious) But isn't that a withdrawal slip?

He puts the slip inside the book and both safely inside his coat pocket.

LANCE. We'll hang onto the book if you don't mind. "Exhibit B", constable.

CATHY. (making a note) Right, Senior.

LANCE hands SAM back her rupees with a satisfied smile.

LANCE. I hope you remember to declare those-rupees on your Australian tax form, madam, and of course report them to the currency control commission. They should be sprayed by customs anyway.

CATHY. (prompting him) And ...

LANCE. (remembers) Oh yes, ah, and in appreciation of your frank admission we'd like to present you with 85 tickets to the police pigeon fanciers jamboree.

CATHY. There's also a squash tournament and sauna thrown in.

LANCE.) Well done.

   ---(applauding together)

CATHY.) Well done.

SAM. Oh thank you very much (smiling weakly, but not quite sure what's going on) Ahm - what did I admit to?

Suddenly there's a familiar CRY OFF in the darkness.

By now the boat has rounded Herron Island and is making its slow way back towards the city

CATHY looks out, "JIM" the skipper puts his spotlight on and picks up a small rubber dingy coming fast at the Yarra Princess from the Como Jetty.

It's LURLENE, she's yelling out from the darkness.

LURLENE.(off) Hey - wait for me!

CATHY. There appears to be some kind of river craft, sir without mandatory navigation lights.

LANCE. Good lord. That's all we need.

CATHY. It appears to be the woman we saw on shore before, sir.

LANCE. Oh very well, constable, go and investigate.

CATHY collects the megaphone and goes out on the
front deck.

CATHY. Over here, madam. Keep rowing, that's the way.

At least this gives LANCE an excuse to demonstrate his mastery of nautical terms.

LANCE Heave to, Skipper. Full ahead reverse thrust, cut engines and wheel about, we'll pull alongside and haul her aboard over.

LURLENE tosses a rope up to CATHY who secures
it and offers LURLENE a hand to clamber aboard.

CATHY. Hold on fast madam, put your oars up, now stow them, that's the way.

Back inside LANCE swings back around on the
audience.

LANCE. Please do not attempt to touch your wallets during this emergency. I've got my eye on you. I want to see those credit cards remain intact!

LURLENE struggles up into the waiting arms of
CONSTABLE WATERMAN, looking somewhat like
a drowned cauliflower, she staggers into the frame of
the front door.

LURLENE. Thought you'd leave me behind did you? Well you can't pull that one. You hired me for four and a half hours and I'm going to see it through. I'm not having me pay docked.

>Concerned, LANCE is trying to help her down the front steps, but she slips and collapses in on top of him, he goes tumbling back as they both roll onto the floor. LANCE quickly finds his feet and his somewhat tattered dignity.

LANCE.)

   (together) Who are you!?

CATHY.)

LURLENE. Lurlene Fowler, what's it to ya?

LANCE. (brushing himself down re-assuming formal command of the situation) I happen to be Senior Sergeant Lance Tippler.

LURLENE. Never heard of ya.

LANCE. Of the Vice, Gaming and Other Expenses Squad.

CATHY. Mounted.

LURLENE. (bit surprise) Ah. So you're the mounted squad?

CATHY. I'm mounted - he's amphibious.

> TAMSIN comes forward closely examining his rigout, she takes one of the long white tubes hanging from his belt, holding it between her hands, examining it closely.

TAMSIN. And yet he clearly has this abiding fear of water. Why, I wonder, does a man choose to work in a job he fears - unless of course he's an insecure, emotional wreck.

LANCE. Would you mind not fondling-my tubes of shark repellent, Doctor. They're likely to go off!

TAMSIN.(retreating quickly) Oh, so you suffer from a premature ejaculation complex do you sergeant?

LANCE jabs his hands onto his hips. He looks just about ready to devour TAMSIN, but is sidetracked again by LURLENE.

LURLENE. Where's that fairheaded fella?

LANCE. Do you mind?

CATHY. Which fairheaded fella?

LURLENE. You know, the one who called me "darling". He made all those fillums and everything.

SAM. He calls everybody darling, darling.

TAMSIN. (quickly seizing another chance) Called - he *called* everybody darling. Made - he *used to* make films.

LANCE explodes.

LANCE. Look, I'm not interested in who called who whom or what! (under his breath) flipping females!

This is too much for CATHY.

CATHY. How dare you say that. You're working with a female.

    LURLENE moves menacingly towards him, fists clenched.

LURLENE. Yeah, bite ya tongue.

    LANCE begins to panic a bit, backing away from both of them.

LANCE. N...n-now, l...l-look girls...

LURLENE.)   We're not girls!
    (emphatically together)
CATHY.)   We're not girls!

LANCE. Alright... alright, ladies ...

CATHY. We're not ladies, we're women.

    Both TAMSIN and SAMANTHA applaud this.

LURLENE. Too right.

LANCE. Well can't we just shake and get on with it (holding out his hand).

CATHY. Who wants to shake hands with you, Lance, it's only a male ritual.

TAMSIN. (mocking) Feeling a little alienated, sergeant ?

LANCE draws CATHY aside.

LANCE. Look, I've been working on his case for years, don't you see?

CATHY. What do you mean "you've been working on it?" I'm the one who broke the case. (she brushes LANCE aside, comes back to LURLENE) Now what about this film-maker?

MICHAEL. Ahm. . . he's out.

TAMSIN. Yes he's *flat*- out.

MICHAEL. ...Working on a script that is - for his next film.

LANCE is almost at boiling point.

LANCE. Look! I'm not interested in *him* - I tell you, I've stumbled onto one of the biggest corporate criminals in Australia! I mean, somewhere on this boat I've - we've - netted (giving the audience a thorough going over) the "Mr. Bottom" of the fraud underworld. I mean somewhere here I'm staring at (staring at them) a promotion to acting Assistant Inspector! (triumphantly)

CATHY. Not in my police force.

LANCE. (including her) And, senior constable (of course).

    LURLENE twigs.

LURLENE. Ah-- so you're after a big crook are ya?

LANCE. (from a certain height) Yes.

LURLENE. (pointing at MICHAEL) Well it's him.

    NIGEL's BLEEPER goes off again. MICHAEL looks nervously at LURLENE, holding out his glass to her

MICHAEL. Could you get me a Bourbon and Berocca Mrs. Fowler. I feel a slight migraine coming on.

CATHY. Everybody freeze!

MICHAEL is stamping his foot around under the table, trying to stop the bleeper.

CATHY. (to MICHAEL) Freeze, I said!

MICHAEL stops. LANCE circles abound him, eying him narrowly.

LANCE. Suffered a little jerk of the knee have we sir? A little twinge in the joints?

MICHAEL edges away.

MICHAEL. Yes... something like that.

Then suddenly he makes a bolt for the front door. LANCE and CATHY rush after him.

LANCE. You'll get more than a twinge in the joints when you go up before the judge this time, pal.

LANCE and CATHY grab MICHAEL just as he's about to make a dive for it into the river to swim away risking not only drowning but toxic shock. They just manage to pull him back inside and then swing him around and face him towards the audience. Caught red handed.

MICHAEL. (starting to crack up) No - I'm sorry, look. No, just leave me out of this. Sorry, went there, did that. (casually) Anyone got a smoke?

LANCE. If you don't mind me saying so, fellow, that's the greatest load of flapdoodle I've ever. heard. (turning back to the audience) What is this? A group booking from Tasmania or something?

CATHY. (on the other side of MICHAEL) Sergeant, will you shut-up and get on with it!

LANCE is stunned.

LANCE. Just who do you think you're talking to, Constable?

CATHY. I'm talking to you, Sergeant, and I'm arresting this man. . .

(grabbing Michael by one shoulder)

LANCE. (cutting in, grabbing his other shoulder) I'm afraid you can't do that, constable. You're out of your jurisdiction.

CATHY. What do you mean?

LANCE. (tugging MICHAEL his way) I'm from South Yarra Station and he's on *my* side of the river. (turns to MICHAEL) Right, Sidney Hart-Lumley I'm arresting you on suspicion of (gross tax fraud).

But CATHY pulls MICHAEL back on to her side of the boat.

CATHY. Well, I'm from Richmond and now he's on my side. (turns to MICHAEL) I'm arresting you for Gross... (tax evasion).

Cleverly LANCE has snuck up behind her and now whips her police hat away.

LANCE. (triumphantly moving away from her) Not without your hat you're not. Sorry - can't arrest anyone without a hat on.

MICHAEL. (sigh of relief) Thank Christ for that.

> MICHAEL moves away from CATHY to get his drink.

MICHAEL. Might just have to fetch that Bourbon and Berocca myself.

LANCE. (to MICHAEL) I'm charging you with Gross Tax Evasion, Scale 1. Misappropriation of Managed Funds, Distortion of Financial Records for Financial Gain and a whole lot of really bad things. Come over here.

CATHY. (through clenched teeth) Give ... me... back ... my ... hat.

LANCE. (holding it away prom her) No.

LURLENE moves menacingly towards him, as before, ready to make it physical.

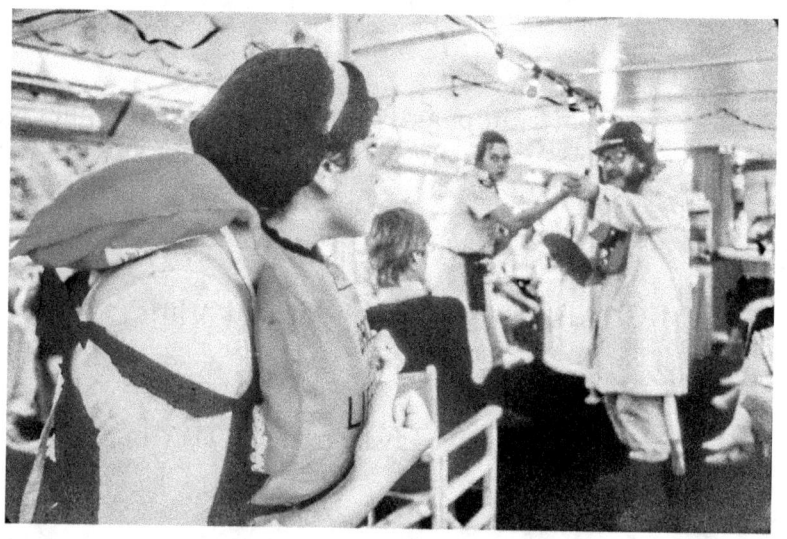

LURLENE. Go on give it back to her.

This gives LANCE pause for thought, he swallows hard. LURLENE can really be quite frightening.

LANCE. Now look - (a natural coward, he's always looking for the easy way out) How about a deal?

CATHY. No deals.

LANCE. Go you halves. (thinking hard) We'll, ah, we'll enter a double charge. You pinch him for domestic violence and I'll nail him for half his liquid assets.

MICHAEL. (quickly skolls his bourbon and puts the empty glass back on the punch table) You might as well take the glass, now pal, because that's about the extent of my liquid assets. As for the violence part of it, well, take a look (indicating SAM) does my ex-wife look at all damaged.

TAMSIN. Not on the surface.

> Of course neither CATHY nor LANCE believe a word of it.

CATHY. Look, I can have him put away for 15 years.

LANCE. I'll have him put away for 20 years.

CATHY. 25 years.

TAMSIN. (low to the audience) I'd have them all put away for life.

> LANCE and CATHY turn to each other.

LANCE.)

        (together) Life!

CATHY.)

That settles it. Nobody can better that. LANCE gives CATHY her hat back. They're united again, a prosecution-winning team. He turns back to MICHAEL

LANCE. Right, you primeval sludge, put your cheque book and major credit cards on the table.

MICHAEL reaches into his inside coat pocket.

LANCE. (yells) Slowly! Ease it down. . . don't rush it! I want to see that balance intact and unadulterated.

MICHAEL carefully puts his chequebook down and scatters a few cards on the table.

LANCE. Now your wallet, bank statements ...

Grudgingly, MICHAEL extracts same and puts them all on the table. LANCE eagerly cleans his glasses with a hankie

LANCE. Mineral futures ... Tertiary bonds...

More paperwork flows out of MICHAEL's clothing and various pockets adding to the pile on the table. Then he stops. Unwilling to go on.

LANCE. And the rest, come on, stolen watches, ladies underwear...

MICHAEL. Come off it. That's your department. (looking at the pile on the table) That's it. Finito la Musica. I suppose this all means I'll have to write off another company or two, sacking the entire workforce without entitlements or any compensation. I hope you walloppers realise the terribly negative effect you're having on unemployment and the economy generally.

LANCE. Don't bullshit me, Sydney. You're a bloody crook, man! I can't believe a word you say.

LANCE stands back from MICHAEL, making way.

LANCE. Right - search him Constable.

CATHY. (bit reluctant) What? A body search? A full 1103?

LANCE. (enjoying his moment of accomplishment) Give the mongrel the works.

> CATHY comes tentatively forward, MICHAEL opens his arms wide. CATHY just barely grazes him and retreats in disarray.

CATHY. Arrrr! No - I can't.

LANCE. Constable, I'm ordering you to-search that villain now! Immediately.

CATHY. (disgusted) I can't. I just can't do it.

LURLENE. Yeah, go on, get him.

TAMSIN. (coming over to assist CATHY, urging her forward) It's alright, dear - never fear. Dr. Tamsin Smythe is here. Dare to touch. Dare to feel. Let your emotions off the reel.

> Acting very professionally TAMSIN "guides" CATHY forward. The young policewoman clenches her eyes shut and protectively thrusts her hands out in front hoping to block MICHAEL away.

TAMSIN. You can, you can do it. Just breathe through it, make contact with your inner self, follow your impulses...

> ...until TAMSIN more or less physically pushes CATHY into MICHAEL.

TAMSIN holds CATHY against MICHAEL while surreptitiously trying to guide CATHY's hands onto MICHAEL's gun.

TAMSIN. Now with your thighs, your cheeks.

CATHY does so, pressing her whole body against MICHAEL's -much to his surprise.

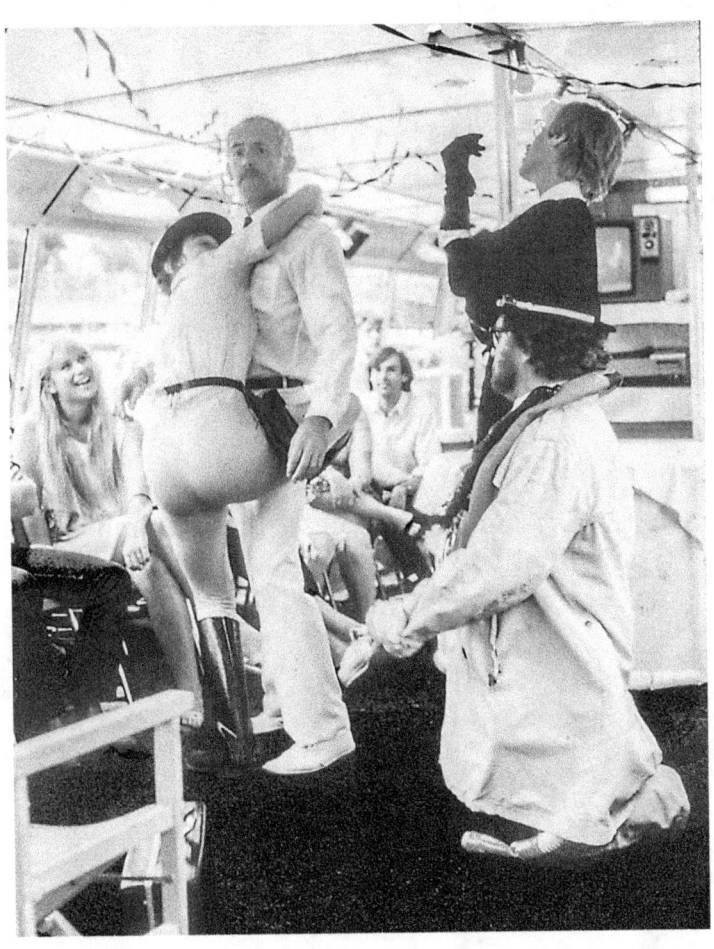

For some strange reason LANCE has dropped to his knees and been urging CATHY on, but pulls up suddenly at this suggestion.

LANCE. (objecting) I don't know about the thighs part!

TAMSIN. Embrace him, embrace it! The solid bit - where his heart should be.

LANCE. (incredulous) Embrace him? That? Hang on a sec...

MICHAEL's has relaxed into enjoying it, but as soon as he feels CATHY is about to press against the pistol in his trouser pocket he suddenly disentangles himself.

MICHAEL. I'm being molested by a member of the Victorian Police Force!

LURLENE. Good. Now you know what it feels like.

MICHAEL. (a sudden flash) I must say it feels ... (rush of sudden admiration) rather wonderful.

CATHY quickly pulls away in disgust, backs off.

MICHAEL. (moving after her) Hi - I'm Sydney. Would you like to have coffee sometime?

LANCE is chasing after MICHAEL who's chasing after CATHY.

LANCE. You'll be lucky if you drink nothing but pigswill for the next twenty five years you blazing yahoo.

MICHAEL. (gazing fondly at her) Couldn't we extend this into a full body search. I am awfully guilty.

LURLENE. shut-up and leave her alone.

Somehow MICHAEL has managed to wrap his arms around TAMSIN on the other side of CATHY while reaching out for her. This mad scrum is pounced upon by LANCE.

MICHAEL. Wednesday nights after five is a good time for me. My number's 8369933.

LANCE tears MICHAEL away and shoves him to one side.

LANCE. Alright, alright. break it up, this isn't "Romper Room" or something. We're attempting to make a serious double arrest here.

LURLENE is hit by a sudden flash of recognition, in the previous fray some of CATHY's hair has fallen down below her cap. The tight policewoman's bun is unraveling.

LURLENE. Hey- aren't you the woman in NIGEL's picture?

LANCE. Who the hell is Nigel?

CATHY. (to LURLENE) Nigel Davidson - the film-maker?

LURLENE. That's the one.

CATHY. Yeah, he used to be an old boyfriend of mine. Unfortunately.

LURLENE squeals with delight.

LURLENE. Isn't that amazing.

CATHY. We shared a flat in Carlton about 8 years ago.

SAM. (with barely disguised disgust) Oh did you really?

LANCE. Look, I'm sorry, but I'm not interested in your romantic biography just now thank you very much.

LURLENE. Pull your hair down.

CATHY. What?

LURLENE. Take off your hat and let your hair down love. Give us a good squizz at ya.

> CATHY does so. Shakes her hair out. LANCE gives up.

LURLENE. See - isn't she the one in the fillums?

TAMSIN. What a transformation.

SAM. Humpf.

MICHAEL. (enraptured) Mygod! You're. . .

SAM. Yes, go on, say it. . .

MICHAEL. (almost kneeling before her) Why you're...

SAM. (sniffling into her hankie) Yes - beautiful, statuesque, adorable, breathtaking, radiant, gorgeous. . .

MICHAEL. Extraordinary! (overwhelmed) What is happening to me? I've never felt like this before.

SAM. How easily you forget, Michael.

MICHAEL. (walking on his knees towards her) My god I'm in ...

CATHY. Keep away.

SAM. I've heard it all before, Michael.

MICHAEL. (to CATHY) Do you by any chance believe in love at first sight?

CATHY just nods, nonchalantly, she's heard it all before too.

SAM. Oh yes, first sight, that's about the extent of it. A quick flash of passion at the beginning quickly followed by years (breaking down again), years of unbearable torture.

LANCE can hold back no longer, as Smantha sniffles into her hankie he assumes control again.

LANCE. Right, stop this touchy feely nonsense and put the cuffs on the grubby little deviate, Constable. We'll grill him up at Russell Street immediately.

CATHY is still keeping her distance from MICHAEL.

CATHY. Look - ah - senior, do I have to?

LANCE. Yes! You are a policewoman first and a man second - (stops, thinks) No, no that's not right...ah...well, something like that.

MICHEL. Couldn't we be handcuffed together?

TAMSIN comes forward offering CATHY her card.

TAMSIN. If you'd like some follow up sessions just call my surgery anytime. I think we had a little breakthrough today, don't you?

CATHY. (as she puts the cuffs on MICHAEL, containing him to a pole in the centre of the boat) Well-- yeah, I suppose...

TAMSIN. If not just send the $200 for the consultation, care of that address.

CATHY. Consultation?

TAMSIN. Yes - the tactile group encounter session we just had.

CATHY didn't realise it was going to cost money.

CATHY. Oh.

LURLENE rounds on MICHAEL now that he's safely handcuffed around one of the poles supporting the boat's roof.

LURLENE. And you - keep your hands to yourself!

In the circumstances MICHAEL can do little else.

LANCE is feeling expansive, now that his job is done.

LANCE.(addressing JIM) Next stop thanks, skipper. We'll call up the dog squad van and take him off in that.

CATHY takes out her pocket radio.

CATHY. K105 to D24 over.

LANCE. (stopping next to the punch, eyeing it thirstily) Tell them operation "floating function" was successful beyond our wildest dreams.

CATHY. (into radio) Request mobile canine detention unit to Swan Street landing, party of one suspect, over.

LANCE. Suspect? (laughs derisively) You're gone pal. (to CATHY) Sweep all that evidence into a bag, Constable, we're going home to a promotion.

> CATHY starts loading bits of damaged furniture, MICHAELs financial documents etc into a black plastic evidence bag.

LANCE. Tell you what, though, it's a dry argument.

> He looks around hopefully, pleasantly.

SAM. I beg your pardon?

LANCE. I say it's thirsty work rooting you beggars out.

> SAMANTHA just stares at him with a strange, quizzical expression.

LANCE. Mind if, ah, you know, I work the wing up and down a bit. . . (bending it) grease the old elbow?

SAM. I'm afraid I haven't the faintest idea of what on earth you're talking about.

LANCE. (suddenly serious, trying to ignore the punch bowl) It's a pretty stiff fine serving grog at a feast like this without a licence.

LURLENE. (ever the translator) I think he wants a drink.

SAM. (realising, ever the hostess) Oh - Oh, yes of course, Inspector.

LANCE likes the sound of the new title, doesn't correct her.

LANCE. Inspector - yes, well it won't be long now. I *will* try a wee dram of that healthy orange juice looking stuff there thanks, Constable.

CATHY. (still collecting evidence) Can't you see I'm busy.

LANCE. Just a little celebratory taste, why don't you have one too, you've earned it.

CATHY. I don't drink on duty.

LANCE. (hurt) It's only orange juice.

SAM. Oh please - don't stint yourselves on our account. (motioning her to do the honours) Mrs. Fowler- if you wouldn't mind...

LURLENE. Wee Wee, Boss.

LANCE. Thank you madam. (taking off his hat making himself comfortable)

LURLENE. Right you are, Mr. Mr.

>While LURLENE pours LANCE a drink, MICHAEL tries to draw CATHY aside, she's working her way past him stuffing relevant bits and pieces into the evidence bag.

MICHAEL. (discretely) Constable, could you come over here for a moment?

CATHY. I'm not going anywhere near you.

MICHAEL. Constable, I've got... I happen to have a terminal illness. I don't actually have a great deal of time left.

CATHY. How disappointing for you.

>LANCE holds his orange juice up to the light, sniffs it, swirls it around and takes a healthy gulp, immediately spasms. (LURLENE has been adding copious amounts of gin to it throughout the evening.)

SAM. Too much guava juice or Staminade, Inspector?

LANCE is fanning his tongue, gasping for air.

LANCE. Puts a shine on your fillings eh? Nothing like a drop of punch to unclog the gums. . .

LANCE goes into automatic fast forward.

LANCE. Yip Yip Yip Ah Ha Ha Swaheeeee!

SAM. Is there something wrong with the punch, Inspector? I mean it's a very simple recipe of my own devising. I take a pinch of nutmeg, a few grams of rosemary tea, some orange juice…

CATHY decides to check the punch herself.

LANCE is fanning himself with his tie, speaks with a hoarse whisper.

LANCE. "Pinch of this"… "Few grams of that!" Madam the thing's 80% proof!!

CATHY. (after a quickly swirling a sample in the test tube she's brought for the purpose) 85.3%, actually. There's enough pure alcohol in there to fuel up a light aircraft. (the crystals in her tube change from blue to red).

LURLENE. Sounds like a pretty good drop to me.

LANCE. (quickly holding his glass out to LURLENE for a refill) Constable. Put a bag on the skipper this instant. If he's over the limit find someone who can drive (quickly skolls his second glass and beats down a gastronomic revolt by pummeling his chest) My god! What if we hit a log, or something awful washed out Melbourne's sewerage system? (sudden panic) We could sink! (he leans against a pole for support) I...I can't swim... I *hate* water: (LANCE collapses down the pole towards the floor) Is there a fog coming down on the river or something? (flat out on the floor, a final manic spasm that goes right along his spine and ends with his heels beating out a crazy tattoo) You'll rot in hell you ginloading bootleggers!!

SAMANTHA makes a stunning, sudden connection. Noticing the same Blue - Yellow - Red stripes.

SAM. You've both got the same tie on!

LANCE's head bobs up from the floor.

LANCE. What?

MICHAEL. What?

They check their ties, look at SAMANTHA, then back at each other. MICHAEL can't believe his luck.

MICHAEL. "Dipsey" Tippler. Geeze you've put on a-bit of a beer gut, mate.

LANCE eyes him narrowly, trying to focus through an instant hangover. Looking down on Michael slightly - or at least trying to. Which isn't easy from the floor.

LANCE. Do I *know* you?

MICHAEL. You remember me: "Snowy Byrne" class of '64. First 8, First 11, SP bookie to the 6th form. You used to get happy sniffing my tranning oil behind the gym.

LANCE struggles to his feet. Still all a bit wobbly from LURLENE's gin infusion.

LANCE. Good Christ!

CATHY. (rounding on MICHAEL, suspicious) I thought you said your name was Lumley?

But MICHAEL's got LANCE in his pocket now.

MICHAEL. Hokatika, eh? Hokatika Hokatika (encouraging LANCE's memory) Wish bang wop...(smacking his knees in turn). Starting a crazy dance.

LANCE slowly picks up MICHAEL's rhythm and joins in
their old school war-cry, smacking knees and
throwing arms into the air together. Starting a strange
primitive gyrating routine.

MICHAEL and LANCE (together)

>Ingo, buddy wuddy give it to ' em 'hot !
>
>Pour the boot,
>
>Pour the boot,
>
>Kick 'em in the head.
>
>Brick a pom,
>
>Trip a wog,
>
>Tank a yank,
>
>Drop 'em like lead
>
>St. Wayne's! St. Wayne's!
>
>Blue - Yellow - Red!

LANCE and MICHAEL LAUGH, high on the
memory of their old school war cry. LANCE goes to
shake hands, but realises MICHAEL's still cuffed to
the pole, and quickly undoes the cuffs.

LANCE. Oh- Sorry to cripple your drinking arm, Sno.

CATHY is appalled.

CATHY. Lance, just what the hell do you think you're doing?

LANCE. It's alright, Constable, Sno's an old St. Wayne's boy. He used to be a Prefect. Strewth, if you can trust a old Christian Brothers' boy the world's in a pretty sordid state.

Behind LANCE's back MICHAEL quickly pulls out a thick leather strap. He swings LANCE around, grabs his hand and holds it out palm facing up, ready to give him six. LANCE looks helpless, terrified, shaking.

MICHAEL. Sorry about this Tippler minor, but it's going to hurt you a lot more than it's going to hurt me, old salt.

Using the end of the strap MICHAEL gently pats LANCE's palm up from underneath to get it higher and easier to hit.

LANCE. (terrified) You can't do this to me!

MICHAEL makes a big lunge with the strap, as if about to smack the blazes out of him, but hits the roof instead with it, making a loud BANG before pulling up short, and LAUGHING. Letting it flop down again.

MICHAEL. Only joking.

At the other end of the boat CATHY is fast running out of patience.

CATHY. Lance!

LANCE. He made me write that war cry out 500 hundred times, you know.

MICHAEL. Did I? (slightly embarrassed)

LANCE. You *were* a prefect.

MICHAEL. Sorry about that.

LANCE. Ah- (dismissive) forget it. I deserved it.

MICHAEL. No, really. it was unforgivable. It was beastly of me.

LANCE. Look - all the Sub-juniors had to do it sooner or later. It built school spirit fercrissake.

MICHAEL. Dipsey, I don't know what to say.

LANCE. (trying to reassure him) Would I remember it now if you hadn't had the gumption to keep me in all weekend writing it out.

MICHAEL. (shrugs) No, I suppose...(not).

CATHY. Lance, can we cut the rugger, pimples and self abuse.

That triggers another memory:

LANCE. Hey, speaking of which, whatever happened to that spasmodic little brunette you took to Hanrahan's 21st, Sno?

CATHY gives up.

MICHAEL. She became my wife.

LANCE takes a slow look back at SAMANTHA, his disappointment with what she now looks like is transparent.

LANCE. Oh god. Did she really?

SAM. I object to that.

MICHAEL. (quickly) But we're divorced now.

LANCE. Oh good - good. phew, eh?

MICHAEL. That reminds me. . . 1965, Doomben cup. Singapore Lady. You still owe me a hundred and twenty, come on, Dipsey, cough up old son.

LANCE reluctantly goes for his wallet.

LANCE. I was kinda hoping you'd forgotten about that.

MICHAEL. (holding out his hand) No way, José.

LANCE starts counting out SAM's rupees, embarrassed that he's kept them.

LANCE. Have to give it to you in, ah foreign notes -sorry...

 LURLENE has a sudden flash.

LURLENE. Singapore!

CATHY. What?

LANCE. What?

MICHAEL. What?

LURLENE. Singapore. That fillumm-maker. He had a bleeper and when it went off he had to ring Singapore. That was just before the gorilla came.

LANCE. What gorilla?

CATHY. What film-maker?

 But LURLENE isn't going to be put off this time. She heads up the front to where the video machine is, takes a tape, examining it.

SAM. (panicked) I think your kettle's on the boil, Mrs. Fowler.

LURLENE. (reading label) Nigel Davidson, see, he made all these fillums - they're all a bit weird, you know. A bit revealing, really.

LANCE. (suddenly. the inspector again, in charge and suspicious) Oh, I get it! Stag movies eh? Nothing like a bit of soft core to go with the illegal punch.

TAMSIN sweeps the video cassette off LURLENE.

TAMSIN. Forheavensake, they're nothing more or less than a harmless collection of family memorabilia. I've been using them as treatment for this poor woman's disordered brain.

LANCE sweeps the cassette off TAMSIN, reads the label.

LANCE. (he manages to make them sound like pornographic titles) "Noosa Honeymoon," "Balwyn Calling," "Draggin Me Backwards" - sounds pretty S & M to me.

SAM. (correcting) S & *N*, actually. "Samantha and Nigel.

LANCE. (still reading labels) And look at this one: "Phallic Symbolism in the early poetry of Derek Abernathy"? That I've got to see.

SAM. It was a perfectly legitimate educational tool that NIGEL made for the English department at Melbourne Uni.

LANCE. Oh- they're *tools* now are they?

TAMSIN sweeps past-and grabs the tape off LANCE again.

TAMSIN. We weren't even proposing to show the thing. it just happened to be on the end of the tape we were using.

CATHY takes the tape off TAMSIN, LANCE spots the whip from among the divorce presents.

LANCE. Oh jawhol, Herr Doktor. (holding up the whip) What do you take me for?

TAMSIN. I don't think you can afford my professional opinion on that.

LANCE. (putting the whip in the evidence bag) With instruments like this, I don't think I want one. (to CATHY) Put the tape on, Constable. I've half a mind to be educated.

TAMSIN. (huffily) Oh well - for half a mind I could probably organise a discount.

CATHY starts the tape.

CATHY. Right, quiet please.

LANCE. (folding his arms) This should be most interesting.

On the screen we see the First Title:

    "Phallic symbolism in the early poetry of Derek Abernathy"

LANCE. ah ha: (takes out his notebook, ready to write)

Then a Second Title appears:

    "Eine arbeit der NIGEL Fassbinderson"

LANCE. oh-- a (meaningfully) *continental* film Constable.

Third Title:

    "For zer national Australian Film Language School (Monetary Studies Department)

LANCE. (writing) "Monetary studies department", no less - this should be *very* interesting. I'm looking forward to this.

> The film starts with a shot of NIGEL in pyjamas standing in a street with a black rectangle of cardboard across his eyes. He reads from a school exercise book.

> Cutaways to various extreme close-ups of SAMANTHA's body jerking in time to the poem:

> eg: Her knees, elbow, thumb.

LURLENE. (identifying NIGEL) That's him! That's Nige.

NIGEL. (on film) "Meanwhile an interstellar space vehicle lands disguised as a rescue helicopter afterall, why panic the humans when it's so much easier to move among them unaware! Loose limbs loop lushingly

into space pauses..."

> LANCE is super sarcastic

LANCE. Educational film, huh? Do you realise the damage these things do to pensioners and children (spitting it out) in the name of "education"!

TAMSIN. I'm sorry - is that dirty? Oh excuse me, I'm only a psychiatrist, of course!

> An obscure close-up of writhing flesh appears.
> Perhaps someone's belly pulsing up and down.

LANCE. What part of the body is that, forgodsake!

MICHAEL. (incredulous, turning to her) Is that *you*, Samantha?

> Back to a shot of NIGEL pyjama-clad, black cardboard obscuring his face.

NIGEL. (on film, reading) "Then the theatre. All shouting from the telegram. Intercepting our earth message from outer space. Trying to give *me* the message that we're onto something different. That the flow is right!

Life force fighting back...

> On "flow" we cut to a garden hose against a yellow wall. Somebody turns the tap on. Water flows out.

> But LANCE can stand it no more. He rushes towards the screen and covers it up with his bowler hat.

LANCE. Oh mygod!

But that's only one screen, there's another one down the other end.

LANCE. Stop! Stop, stop the film!

CATHY does so, pressing the eject button.

SAM. I did warn him not to use that shot.

MICHAEL. (disappointed) It was just getting mildly interesting.

LANCE. Show me that filth, thank you, Constable.

CATHY brings the tape over to LANCE who glances again at the label.

LANCE. (reading) "S & N blue light movie club."

SAM. See I told you.

CATHY. Do you have an exhibition licence for this trash?

SAM. (confidently) We don't need one.

LANCE. I beg your pardon.

SAM. Everyone here's a member. It was a strictly private screening, until you two blundered in.

CATHY. You have proof of this?

SAM. They all signed the book. (indicating her guests) Didn't you?

ALL. Yairs.

LANCE. Which book?

SAM. (pointing down the back) Over there.

LANCE and CATHY race for the book, she pips him at the post, LANCE slams his palm into his fist again in frustration.

CATHY. (holding it up) You're saying all their names and addresses are in this book?

SAM. Every single one of them.

LANCE. Right, confiscate the book constable (since she's beaten him to it), and when you get back to Russell street (he includes the whole boat) put them all down for an intensive retrospective tax records check!

SAM. (shocked) What? (her party is really falling apart)

LANCE. You'll all be getting your summonses in the mail.

TAMSIN. (protesting) But these good people are all decent, upright, members of Balwyn and the greater Camberwell community. You've only got to look at their addresses - they're absolutely impeccable.

LANCE leans triumphantly on the wedding cane. The hole that SAMANTHA came out of has been covered with a table cloth.

LANCE. Oh yeah, doc? Well they don't look too upright to meeeeeeee! (his hand slides sideways and he tumbles head first into the cake).

The cake is next to the table under which NIGEL has been hidden. The sight of LANCE tumbling in on top of him shocks NIGEL back to life. LANCE is equally startled to find a body under there. Their SCREAMS coincide.

LANCE.)

        Ahhhhhhhh

NIGEL)

LANCE's feet dangle absurdly up through the hole, they slowly disappear as NIGEL crawls out from under the other end of the table.

NIGEL. (holding his head, not sure if he's alive or dead) Is this Hollywood?

LURLENE. There he is!

SAMANTHA rushes over and smothers him with kisses.

SAM. Nigel, Nigel, you're alive! I'm *soooo* happy, I thought this might have

affected our relationship.

MICHAEL. Neville, I never thought I'd be so pleased to see you.

TAMSIN. (happily) Yes, you'll be back on my couch in no time.

And finally:

CATHY. (calmly, with restraint) Hullo, Nigel.

NIGEL. (turns, stunned) CATHY!

CATHY. Well, well, well...

NIGEL. (with obvious distaste) What ? You're a cop? What happened to your job at "Bubbles" ?

CATHY. You owe me $3000 maintenance, *mate*!

NIGEL. (blank) Huh?

CATHY. Twelve months and not a cent off you, Nigel! (almost screaming at him).

NIGEL reaches out for her, trying to calm her down.

NIGEL. Now, look, ah. . . Cathy, I can explain everything. . .

LANCE's head protrudes from under the table. He spots NIGEL with his hands groping towards CATHY and rises up between them.

LANCE. (flinging NIGEL away) Get your hands off her you filth!

But in doing so LANCE rips NIGEL's shirt open and about 20 pairs of dice fall out. LANCE can't believe the extent of the crime he's uncovering.

LANCE. Dice (holding it up, they're falling everywhere) Dice!

NIGEL. (to CATHY, still can't believe it) You? a cop? The last time I saw you you were working for an escort agency.

CATHY. That was an undercover job.

As NIGEL and CATHY continue to catch up on old times LANCE swaggers gleefully around the boat, pointing to the material evidence of the different crimes.

LANCE. That's illegal gambling,. . . alcohol in the punch...

NIGEL. But ... you're really a cop?

CATHY. Well I had to work didn't I, we'd be starving waiting for your parental support payments.

SAM. What support payments?

LANCE. (still counting them off) Pornographic films, gross tax evasion.... driving a public water conveyance under the influence...probably drugs...

NIGEL. Look Samantha, Cathy and me... it was a long time ago, ok ? A lot of film's gone through the gate...

LANCE blows his whistle. Things come to a halt.

LANCE. (yells - quite drunk now) Right! Arrest everybody!

NIGEL is on his knees picking up the scattered dice.

NIGEL. Forgodsake,they were only props, I tell you. For my next film clip.

LANCE. (to CATHY) Cuff yourself to that demented prefect constable.

(indicating MICHAEL)

CATHY. I'm past caring for you Nigel. (as she cuffs herself to MICHAEL).

MICHAEL. Eh? (turning to him) What about the "Ingo buddy, wuddy wish bang wop" Lance?

LANCE. Out the window, pal. You're gone son.

NIGEL. But, CATHY, I pulled focus on our relationhship because I didn't want to bring you down with me.

SAM. (news to her) Oh really, is that how you describe it?

While LANCE takes the opportunity of replenishing his hip-flask from the punch bowl.

And amidst the chaos, LURLENE tries to make sense of it all:

LURLENE. So you (NIGEL) were with her (CATHY) and you (SAMANTHA) were with him (MICHAEL) now she's

(CATHY) with you (MICHAEL) (since they're cuffed together) and you're (SAMANTHA) with

him (NIGEL). (to NIGEL) Are you married?

NIGEL. Are you kidding?

TAMSIN. Don't worry, Mrs. Fowler, this kind of thing happens quite a lot in North Balwyn.

CATHY checks the landscape out through a window.

CATHY. We're coming up to the Swan street landing, Senior.

LANCE quickly closes his whisky flask and stands up, guilty about being caught at it.

LANCE. (peering out with her) Oh, Er…right - can you see the divvy van? (looking around at them) We'll need a bus as well for this lot.

Pull over, skipper.

MICHAEL quickly pulls out his gun, points it straight at LANCE.

MICHAEL. Not so fast, Dipsey.

There's a tense pause. Everyone freezes.

CATHY. What?

LANCE. (cavalier, LAUGHS outright) Don't think you can threaten me, Byrne. You're going to dance from the yard-arm 'ere this night is through.

LURLENE is equally unphased.

LURLENE. The moment I laid eyes on you I knew you were a rotten egg.

MICHAEL fires a warning shot through the roof. This stuns everyone back into line. He points the weapon directly at LANCE who's trying to hide behind LURLENE.

MICHAEL. (sudden manic threat) Shut-up all of you or I'll splatter his (LANCE's) cerebellii all over the people sitting directly behind him.

LANCE's hands shoot up so fast he hits the ceiling, groans in pain, bends over double, shaking his wounded wrist, then quickly straightens and holds his hands up again.

SAM. (sweetly, but with her sanity wavering) Michael, I haven't changed into my going away outfit, yet.

MICHAEL. The only person going anywhere, Samantha, is him (shaking the gun at LANCE) and he's going straight down.

There's a gasp of horror from LANCE, but he's too scared to speak. MICHAEL indicates the black plastic bags, the wet briefcase etc. that LANCE claimed had been found in the river trawling behind the boat.

MICHAEL. Is that all the evidence you've collected?

CATHY. Yes, I should think so.

MICHAEL. Well, load him up, Neville.

NIGEL would like to protest, but the gun's pointed at him now.

NIGEL. (as he throws the bags around LANCE's neck, weighing him down) Look, I want you to know I'm only doing this under duress, given more time we'd probably get to like each other.

LANCE. (weepy with fear) Oh sure.

MICHAEL. Right, that should keep him on the bottom for a good 20 minutes or so.

LURLENE. If your mother could see you now.

MICHAEL. Shut-up!

> LANCE starts to panic

LANCE. (pleading - pathetically) Now, listen, Sno, Mickey, me old cock, me old china... ah, plate.

MICHAEL. Don't you "old-mate" me you scumbag. Give us the-keys to the cuffs.

> Despite his predicament, that's a bit much for
> LANCE. He fumbles in his pockets for the key,
> managing to always keep one hand up.

CATHY. Quickly, Lance.

> Finally and a bit reluctantly he locates them, holds
> them up, the keys rattling, his hand shaking.

MICHAEL. (from down the front) Pass them over here.

> LANCE goes to throw the keys forward, but just can't
> bring himself to do it. Instead he chucks them out an
> open window, They quickly sink.

LANCE and LURLENE think that's a huge joke. They LAUGH uproariously. Then as they settle a little, LANCE confident he's had the last laugh:

LANCE. (laughs) Dive for it, scumbag!

MICHAEL. Are they the same keys as for your cuffs? (noticing the cuffs on LANCE's life saving vest)

LANCE. Yes. ah ha ha ha ha (laughs).

LURLENE joins in, a real knee slapping job.

MICHAEL. Well cuff yourself to the old boiler then.

The smiles drop. It's back to blind panic again.

LANCE. Hey, no listen, Mickey. . . heck... we don't wanta cause any trouble, right? We don't wanta.

MICHAEL (again the manic yell) Just bloody well *DO-IT*!

LANCE crumbles immediately.

LANCE. (cuffing himself to LURLENE) Oh- of course, yes sir, anything you say. . . sir

LURLENE. (to MICHAEL) You bastard!

SAMANTHA, declining rapidly, has retreated back to the cake, she sits inside it with just her head sticking out.

SAM. Michael, I simply have to go home, darling. The cleaners are coming tomorrow and I must mess up the lounge a bit.

MICHAEL. Shut-up!

SAM. You know I only agreed to move from South Yarra to Balwyn because little Sasha was mixing with poddles who took drugs.

TAMSIN. (shouting) That's probably why he's got a pulmonary embolism!

SAMANTHA in her nervousness tries to light her cigarette holder.

LANCE summons up his last reserves of cowardice. If he's going to walk the plank then he's got nothing left to lose.

LANCE. There's no reasoning with him, madam. Alas, the criminal mind is beyond the call of logic I'm afraid.

TAMSIN. So many amateur psychiatrists, I can't believe it.

SAM. (from the cake) Who keeps blowing out my cigarette lighter?

By now LANCE too, has snapped, he's round the twist.

LANCE. Oh yes, yes, how the mighty have fallen on thee, sweet Jericho!

What? Who said that? He asked as the autumn wavered on the point of

midnight.

   He quickly drops his face in the punch, starts blowing bubbles.

LANCE. Ahh-- that's cooler. I was only a scholarship lad myself.

CATHY. Lance, will you pull yourself together, this is serious.

LANCE. (defensive) I'm a member of the public too, you know. You can't tell me where to read my poetry.

MICHAEL. Try underwater for a change. Now move it!

LANCE. It's unconstitutional I tell you.

MICHAEL. Not since 1975.

   As MICHAEL pushes LANCE and LURLENE towards the door.

LANCE. Righto Byrne, take your coat off. Come on, fight like a man.

LANCE and LURLENE walk backwards around the boat - pushed on by MICHAEL and CATHY: the-two sets of handcuffed couples.

LANCE. Listen, Sno I hate water. You know I never made the rowing team.

MICHAEL. Well,- now you're well and truly up the creek without a paddle, Dipsey, sorry, but ... you're taking the fall.

Dragging LURLENE with him, LANCE tries to hold on things - onto people, anything to postpone the inevitable. As MICHAEL continues to push them forward towards the front door:

LURLENE. (stops for a moment, standing her ground) What about my pay? I'm entitled to two hours casual rates and one hour-over time and danger money. I'm entitled to danger money.

MICHAEL. Don't give me that union claptrap. Get into the raft. You're lucky I'm giving you a sporting chance.

LANCE is desperate. he stops from mopping his brow and dangles his hankie in front of MICHAEL like a flag of surrender.

LANCE. Sno, sno mate (quoting the song) "We're not waiting for the world to bring us together" Sno. It's ..."It's time to turn on the lights!"

> Undeterred, MICHAEL continues to push LANCE and LURLENE towards the front door of the boat and the waiting life raft that LURLENE only recently arrived on.

NIGEL. (aside to the audience) Are there any heroes on board? Do you think I should film this?

> LURLENE makes one last try:

LURLENE. What about my clothes? I can't go home on the train looking like this.

SAM. If you could drop the cossie into a dry cleaners then pop it in a post bag to us, Mrs. fowler. Thank you so much for all your help.

MICHAEL. (waving his pistol at them) Right - in the raft.

> LURLENE and LANCE stumble into her rubber raft.

LANCE. Cathy, Constable waterman, help!

CATHY. Why don't you just fire your distress pistol.

LANCE. I'm warning you, Byrne, I'm calling for a Royal Commission over this. You're all under arrest! I've got your names and addresses, (looks around him, the book they signed is missing). Stop, stop laughing, the man's an absolute scallywag. He even stole a bag of marbles off me in primary school.

>LANCE and LURLENE half stumble, half fall into her rubber raft and CATHY casts them off, throwing the rope after them. Out in the dark, LANCE's rantings and LURLENE's screams of protest become fainter as they drift off into me night. LANCE stands awkwardly in the wildly rocking rubber raft, almost capsizing the thing He vainly tries to get the oars working. But in making for the shore he merely succeeds in making the thing go round and round in circles. We slowly leave their predicament behind as the MV *"Yarra Princess"* sails on.

LANCE.(a last strangled cry) Come back, *Yarra Princess!* Return here immediately.

SAM. (sweetly) Bye bye, Inspector.

>MICHAEL comes back inside the boat looking smug and rather satisfied with himself.

>He hangs there a moment, thinks for a bit, then:

MICHAEL. Just a minute, I've forgotten something...

>He moves quickly turns and moves outside onto the deck again and quickly fires off TWO SHOTS in the direction of LANCE and LURLENE's raft.

MICHAEL. (irritated) Stand still! (fires a third shot)

MICHAEL comes back in, reloading his pistol.

MICHAEL. Don't know whether I punctured the thing or not. Mrs. Fowler was weaving around all over the place.

CATHY spots LANCE's bowler where it had fallen off during the tumble into the cake. For a moment she goes a bit sentimental.

CATHY. Poor Lance.

MICHAEL. You want to go back to him ? (very much doubting it).

CATHY. (sighs) No. Not really. (sudden rage of frustration) Gawd I'm *sick to death* ! of the way he carries on sometimes but... (changes again, shrugs) I need the job, you know. That's not old fashioned is it? What other support can a single mum count on?

MICHAEL. (gallantly) I'll look after you.

TAMSIN. Ohgod! I'm going to need a drink.

NIGEL. (still feeling guilty/jealous) Cathy, you've got to understand why I left that time.

CATHY. I'll give you three reasons why you left NIGEL. (counting on her fingers) One, you're too selfish.

NIGEL. Alright. alright. . .

CATHY. Two, you're too selfish.

NIGEL. Okay, I get it...

CATHY.) And three,

CATHY)   You're too selfish.

    (together)--

NIGEL.)   You're too selfish

NIGEL. You're right.

SAM. And he's shy, too. He's very, very shy.

NIGEL. (to CATHY) But things are different now.

CATHY. Sure. (heard it all before)

NIGEL. I'm telling you, I've got this fabulous idea for a bush crime story. .

CATHY. (warning) NIGEL!

NIGEL. ... told from a whole lotta points of view - the victim's view, the aboriginal view, the other campers. . .Like the *Seven Samuari*...

    MICHAEL is hit by a powerful thought.

MICHAEL. You're doing the Azaria Chamberlain story!

NIGEL. No. (quick reverse) What? I never said that. (too quickly)

MICHAEL. *"Desperate Convictions"*. I've got money in that film.

NIGEL. You what?

SAM. (news to her) What?

MICHAEL. My broker added it to my investment portfolio last week.

SAM. (sarcastic) Oh did he, that was nice of him. My lawyers certainly didn't know about that little nest egg.

NIGEL. Samantha, can't you see what he's done? The telephone calls from Singapore. The mini golf-link in Surfers that suddenly won't sell? He thought by sabotaging our film deal he could sabotage our relationship.

MICHAEL. You've got to admit it was a sound idea. Trouble is...in the process I went broke as well.

SAM. Oh you bloody fool, you bloody, bloody fool!

NIGEL. Isn't there any Hong Kong money you can borrow against?

MICHAEL. Sorry, old chum - it all went down the canal at Noosa.

In another corner, TAMSIN is quietly getting sloshed. NIGEL decides he might as well join her.

NIGEL. I feel sick.

TAMSIN. Have another drink, Nigel, darling.

MICHAEL. I'm afraid all I've got left is the hundred and twenty I won off Lance and the two tickets to LA.

NIGEL. (outraged) She gave you those tickets for little Sasha!

MICHAEL. I dropped him at your place on the way over, Samantha. There's nothing wrong with him. You always were his favourite anyway. Sorry about the little fib. . . (shrugs) I suppose I was trying to hurt you as much as I (deep breath)... felt you'd hurt me. But all that's over now. Now that I feel (looks to CATHY) bound to someone else.

CATHY. (news to her) What?!

MICHAEL. I can't promise anything, but if you'd like to come with me we could be in LA by Tuesday.

CATHY thinks about it.

CATHY. I think I'd really prefer New York.

MICHAEL. I'll take you anywhere, anywhere, I'll even marry you, if you want me to.

TAMSIN. Oh surely you're joking.

This puts SAMANTHA into hysterics. She starts hyperventilating.

NIGEL. It's a bit like swapping deck chairs on the Titanic at this stage, isn't it?

But MICHAEL is only interested in CATHY's reaction.

MICHAEL. Can't you see this is love at first sight? That beneath this sham materialism there lies genuine, human emotions?

NIGEL. Oh *come* on!

CATHY. (tempted) I suppose we are already legally linked (looking at the cuffs). We could make a virtue of a necessity... but we may not have that much time...to...to... (get married)

MICHAEL. (bright idea) We're on a boat aren't we? The skipper can marry us! Right of the sea.

JIM. This is *not* the "Love Boat."

NIGEL. Oh now, this is truly absurd!

SAM. Oh why don't you marry them, Tammy. You're a registered marriage celebrant.

MICHAEL. (new hope) Are you?

TAMSIN. I wish you hadn't mentioned that, Samantha. I mean, look at me! This is the first drink I've had in seven years! Look what your blasted therapy's driven me to.

NIGEL. Cathy, look around you, can't you see what a trap marriage is?

CATHY, admittedly, does have second thoughts.

CATHY. It *is* all a bit sudden.

MICHAEL. (expansively) Embrace the moment, Catherine. Hug life. Break free of your old fetters...

CATHY. It's just that, well marriage is for life isn't it?

SAMANTHA laughs outright.

SAM. Darling, "life" for Michael is about 15 years - or less, with 5 years' remission for bad behaviour.

MICHAEL. Alright, alright, I'm not infallible. Don't take me forever. It's only a contract isn't it? We'll write a special termination clause. Make it 8 years, 7 ... make it till the first seven year itch.

TAMSIN. (becoming more reckless as the alcohol takes over) Why not do yourselves a favour and make it seven seconds. (laughs uproariously)

A joke! I make a joke! (giggles impulsively, hiccupping alcohol) I ... (as if realizing for the first time) I've got a sense of humour! Ha. (laughs hysterically)

CATHY. Yeah, but it's not proper is it? I mean it's on a boat and everything.

MICHAEL. Are you kidding? We've got a cake, we've got party lights, guests, presents, alcohol, it's all set, ready to go...

SAM. (protesting) I *paid* for this party.

MICHAEL. With money stolen from me.

TAMSIN. (suddenly sober, and angry) She didn't steal it. The judge give it to her in court this morning. You lost it the same way you lost everything else.

MICHAEL rummages in his pockets.

MICHAEL. Alright, alright, to hell with it. Here, look (counting contents of his wallet) I've got 60, 80, 120 Rupees (slams them on the table) I'll buy what's left of the party. And you can keep the deposit on the gorillagram suit.

CATHY. (still having second thoughts) Yeah, but it's just that I don't know about the kids. . . I can't just fly off to New York and leave them. They're still in primary school.

This pulls MICHAEL up short.

MICHAEL. Kids? You've got kids?

CATHY. Yeah.

MICHAEL. How . . . ah many?

CATHY. Two. Boys.

MICHAEL swallows hard. TAMSIN laughs.

TAMSIN. That's taken the puff out of his sails.

MICHAEL Look, ahm, Cathy - could we, you know, about that contract, could we settle on say maybe just a couple of years . . ?

CATHY. Well...

MICHAEL. (looking for a way out) Of course if you have to check with the father. . .

NIGEL. Well, that's me, pal. One of those boys is mine.

MICHAEL. Oh. (tentative) Could we make it 12 months ? (winces).

CATHY. Six.

MICHAEL. (eagerly) Done.

They shake.

NIGEL. Cathy, Cathy are you mad!? Daryl will never get on with him.

CATHY. How would you know? You've hardly even seen the kid. You didn't know he existed till we bumped into each other on that tram last year.

MICHAEL. Righto, Tammy, do your stuff.

TAMSIN. I'm sorry, but I cannot in anyway assist with this bizarre liaison.

MICHAEL. (pointing the gun directly at her) Now look, Smythe, you saw the dollar signs light up when Samantha walked into your clinic. You'll sell people out if it suits you.

TAMSIN. (nudging the pistol away from her direction a little) I certainly will not be bludgeoned into any shot-gun wedding.

MICHAEL. It's not you I want to marry. And its only a pistol.

    NIGEL is holding his ears.

NIGEL. I don't believe this. It's like the river trip in *"Apocalypse Now"*.

Reluctantly TAMSIN takes some standard marriage forms out of her briefcase.

CATHY. Will you shut-up Nigel. I'm 31, I've got two kids to clothe and feed, offers of marriage aren't something that happen every other day.

But in fact she *is* ready for it, takes a cake cover from one of the food talbles and puts it over her head like a bridal veil. TAMSIN puts the wedding march music on the cassette recorder. at the same time the credits for people involved in the production of the play start to scroll automatically across the video screen.

TAMSIN. Dear friends, we are gathered here today to witness the holy vows of matrimony.

NIGEL. (biting his fist) Oh the horror, horror, horror...

TAMSIN. (continued) . . . between these two young people who give themselves freely one to the other.

NIGEL. I feel like Humphrey Bogart in "*Africa Queen*".

SAM. (out of nowhere) My buckettes party!

TAMSIN. What?

SAM. I suddenly had a flash of my buckettes party. Tamsin, it's, it's, all coming back to me.

TAMSIN. Not now, darling.

MICHAEL. Can we get on with it?

TAMSIN. (turning to her) Do you Cathy…

CATHY. May

TAMSIN. May

CATHY. Waterman.

TAMSIN. Waterman. Take this. . . (looking, him up and down) shit to be your lawful wedded thing?

SAMANTHA SCREAMS

SAMANTHA. Oh no - I'm beginning to see the whole ghastly detail.

TAMSIN. It's rather inconvenient just now, Samantha.

SAM. My w. . .w...wedding, the whole m... m... marriage is coming b... b...b back to m m m me.

NIGEL. That's easy for you to say, Samantha. I'm looking at the mother of my only child going off with a complete animal.

MICHAEL. I'll have you know, Neville, it's people like me have made this country what it is today.

TAMSIN.(continuing regardless) To have and to hold, to cherish and obey, in sickness and health. . .

CATHY. That's a bit much.

TAMSIN. What?

CATHY. The obey part - don't know about "obey".

They look to MICHAEL.

MICHAEL. (shrugs) I only want you to be happy, darling.

TAMSIN crosses out the clause about "obey", hands the biro and contract to CATHY.

TAMSIN. Just initial the changes.

CATHY does so, hands them back to TAMSIN.

TAMSIN. (reading again) With this body I thee worship.

There's immediate objection to this down the back.

NIGEL. Whaaatt?

SAM. Oh surely not, doctor,

MICHAEL eagerly takes biro and contract.

MICHAEL. I'll initial that.

TAMSIN. To have and to hold, to cherish and disobey, in sickness and in health, until six months do you part. '

CATHY (eagerly - her dream come true) I do.

NIGEL. (a pathetic wail) Caaaathhhyyyyy!

TAMSIN. Do you Michael, Reginald, Rupert, Fitzwilliam Hart-Byrne (aka) Sidney Lumly, aka Richard Tatianko, aka Morrie Cummins) take...

MICHAEL. (brusquely) Yes, yes, where do I sign?

NIGEL. (plucking at straws) Cathy, CATHY! He's only doing it to neutralise your evidence. Can't you see that? Once you're married it's inadmissable.

TAMSIN. Is there anybody here knows any reason why these two people should not be wed?

NIGEL. Know any reason? How many do you want?

MICHAEL. (to TAMSIN) Come on, come on, we've got a plane to catch.

NIGEL. Are you listening to me?

TAMSIN. Nigel, just settle down! Can't you see I've got a gun pointing at my left temporal lobe?

NIGEL staggers up to the happy couple and collapses on his knees in front of CATHY.

NIGEL But Cathy, I loooooooovvvveeee you!

She knees him in the groin, NIGEL collapses backwards.

SAM. (lying down on the table as if on TAMSIN's couch) I've just taken 24 Mogodon. I think that's a record… I only wanted to say good-bye.

TAMSIN. (to MICHAEL) Have you got the ring?

SAM. And then Father Murphy got tanked with Mummy and

cut his finger on some wire from one of the bridesmaid's bouquets.

MICHAEL. (back to TAMSIN) What?

TAMSIN The ring?

MICHAEL. Oh hell-

SAMANTHA stretches herself out on the floor.

SAM. (trills) I'm' ready now doctor, I'm waiting...

MICHAEL rushes up to SAMANTHA and roughly pulls a ring off one of her fingers.

SAM. I *do* father, yes, I do I do I do-do-de-do...
(sings) Raindrops keep falling on my head....

Needless to say SAM has gone completely bonkers.

MICHAEL (still handcuffed) drags CATHY back up o to TAMSIN.

MICHAEL. Right (pushing SAMANTHA's ring on CATHY) It doesn't quite... (fit)

CATHY. Ow.

MICHAEL. Little finger.

She offers it and he finally shoves it on. Cathy happily displays the ring for all to see.

NIGEL moves up where SAMANTHA is lying, and drops down beside her, he wants to lie down too. Adopts a foetal position.

By now conversations start to overlap:

NIGEL. It's like that first journey down the fallopian tube. . . the two halves of the brain, the two banks of the river. I am Moses in the bullrushes.

SAM. (sitting bolt upright) Excuse me, this is my haberdashery shop.

TAMSIN. (almost spitting it out) I now pronounce you "woman" and "object".

> Overjoyed, MICHAEL goes to kiss CATHY. She pulls back.

CATHY. Don't kiss me - I've got a cold sore.

> TAMSIN snaps her book shut and moves down to kneel between her two patients.

TAMSIN. Now come Samantha, tell me all about it, darling

SAM. We honeymooned in the Windsor, yes.

TAMSIN. Yes ? (go on)

SAM. And there was a bottle of pink bubbly in the fridge and a bowl of iced vovos...

TAMSIN. I think she's got it. By George, she's got it!

> NIGEL gets up and starts putting on MICHAEL's gorilla costume. SAMANTHA seems to come out of her dream - only it's a nightmare.

SAM. Oh no ! Oh no! I'm married! (appalled)

> MICHAEL and CATHY go around the boat, still handcuffed but thanking everyone for coming to their wedding. It's been lovely to see them all.

TAMSIN. (slapping her about a bit) SAMANTHA! wake up. It's alright, you're *free* Samantha. The *decree nisi* came through this morning. Just after you got back from Denpasar.

SAM. (blearily lifting herself off the floor) What? (vaguely looking round) Where am I?

TAMSIN. You and NIGEL have a happy and preposterous - er...prosperous de facto relationship.

SAM. Who's Nigel?

TAMSIN. Oh no- (slapping her forehead: here we go again)

SAM. I haven't been to Cairo for ages, I'd love to come.

TAMSIN.(swinging her round to face her square on) Samantha! Look at me. Which - Samantha - am - I - talking - to?

> MICHAEL comes up to TAMSIN.

MICHAEL. (sheepishly robbing her handbag at gun point) Listen, doc, I'm sorry about this, but I need a little folding stuff for the taxi to the airport.

> The *MV Yarra Princess* comes slowly back into Princes Walk landing where the whole
>
> divorce celebration began.

> Pocketing TAMSIN'S cash, MICHAEL's ushers his new wife CATHY towards the front door.
>
> CATHY indicates that she wants to be carried through the door.

CATHY. Aren't you going to...

MICHAEL. (slumping at the prospect) Ah what?

CATHY. I've always wanted to.

> So MICHAEL tries to pick CATHY up, to carry her out through the door but just can't quite manage it. Drops her down again.

MICHAEL. Sorry, love, it's me back, you know.

> As soon as the boat docks and JIM throws a rope onto the jetty MICHAEL and CATHY are out through the

door. They race off into the night, quickly disappearing towards Swanston Street.

MICHAEL. Taxi! taxi!

TAMSIN turns to the guests who are left.

TAMSIN. Thank you so much for coming this evening, ladies and gentlemen. As you can see, my therapy has been spectacularly successful beyond my wildest dreams. I can confidently predict now that Samantha has recovered her full memory of that awful day she married Michael Hart-Byrne. Unfortunately, she ...(a touch sheepish) she seems to have forgotten just about everything, else. Since. (on brighter note) However I don't see any real problem there. . .Another 18 months or so of therapy should soon find some closure. One hopes.

By now NIGEL is fully decked out in Michael's gorilla suit.

NIGEL. Hey, doc, I've got this great idea for a feature film: it starts with

divorce and it ends in marriage.

SAM. I said the toilet's blocked.

NIGEL. It'll be from different points of view: the bride's view, the psychiatrist's view, the yeti's view.

TAMSIN marches straight up to him, slaps him hard and shakes him vigorously by the shoulders.

TAMSIN. Nigel! Come back to your normal 32 years of age and go and bash a pillow for 10 minutes.

NIGEL looks stung. Humble. He holds his jaw, feeling the slap.

TAMSIN gently takes both NIGEL and SAMANTHA by the hand and leads them, like submissive children towards the door.

TAMSIN. Can't you see, Samantha, Nigel can't make his films unless he's slightly mad. And he thinks that if I cure him, he'll lose his creativity.

NIGEL. Actually I'm giving up film making. I think I'll become a hairdresser.

TAMSIN. (moving with NIGEL and SAMANTHA up out of the boat) That's why you need me, Nigel. That's why you both need me.

Mysteriously the title:

"THE END"

comes up on the video as the guests file out.

Written with the assistance of a Playwright in Residence grant from the Literature and Theatre Boards of the Australia Council - a statutory body of the Commonwealth Government. Produced with the assistance of the Victorian Ministry for the Arts

CRITICAL RECEPTION

Theatre for the people is afloat!

PEOPLE by Di Lyttleton

MOST people's private lives are very private but North Balwyn celebrity Samantha Hart-Byrne wants everyone to come to a party to celebrate her divorce from Michael Hart-Byrne, Flemington punter and well known tax minimiser.

Samantha and her boyfriend Nigel Davidson, an independent Sydney film-maker, are holding the party on a ferry, the Yarra Princess, which leaves from Princes Bridge and travels upstream past the murky gloom of Como Island.

There will be music, dancing and some of Nigel's films and the party promises to do for divorce what Dimboola did for marriage.

The party is actually a play, Breaking Up In Balwyn, and the audience will be expected to survive a raid by the Vice, Gaming and Other Expenses Squad and return from the trip quite sane.

A satire on money, marriage and divorce, it is by Theatre Works, the same group who put on Storming Mont Albert By Tram, in a tram, last year.

Both plays are the work of Paul Davies, a writer who believes in community involvement. Paul got the idea for the tram show when he was sitting in a tram and two men were arrested by police for causing a disturbance.

Trams

"It occurred to me," he explained, "that theatre was happening on trams all the time and I just recreated it. The boat show grew out of the tram show because, in the second half of the tram journey, Samantha invited everyone back to her house for a party but she was arrested before the journey ended.

"It's the same cast in both plays," Paul added. He is also a member of the cast but insists he is a writer first, an actor second.

"In both shows the passengers-cum-audience are invited guests with actors salted in amongst them. There is no division, which enhances the comedy and generates excitement. It is hard for people to avoid being involved and they tend to talk back to the cast. They are not pressurised to react but the option is there.

"Obviously, because of this, the actors must be able to improvise and invent material within the character they are playing.

"We had a classic situation with the tram where a chap missed the start and caught a taxi to catch up. The cabbie kept beeping but we were almost in the city before he was able to stop the tram and board. When he got on he then had to find his friends to borrow money because he couldn't pay the fare and the cab kept following. It all became part of the show.

"A 'Special' sign was on the front of the tram but, at times, when we stopped to pick up actors on the way people got on by mistake. Some stayed on, others got off.

"Every night something different happened which was great for us because it never got stale. One night there was a crush in front of the tram and it had to detour which put us off our schedule but we improvised madly. People thought the stage would be down one end of the tram but the journey was the play.

"The boat trip will be similar with actors getting on and off at various little jettys.

Captain Peter Grantidis of the Yarra Princess and writer Paul Davies.

Storming the Yarra by boat

ONE of the most enterprising theatre shows last year in Melbourne was 'Storming Mont Albert by Tram', a piece of mobile theatre staged aboard a tram travelling from the depths of Mont Albert to the city.

Using the same formula the group responsible, Theatre Works, has now devised a sequel, 'Breaking Up in Balwyn', performed aboard a Yarra riverboat.

The ostensible purpose of the two-hour river cruise, which begins and ends at Princes Walk, is to celebrate the divorce of a rich spoilt Balwynite, one Samantha Hart-Byrne (Hannie Rayson).

After five years of misery with husband Michael (Peter Sommerfeld), a wealthy tax minimiser and man about town, Samantha has finally won her freedom.

She ought to be happy; but no.

THEATRE
Leonard Radic

The beginning of the party sees her in a doleful mood, and in need of consolation from her on-the-spot psychiatrist (Susie Fraser).

The analyst is something of a red herring in Paul Davies's script. My instinct would be to play her down, and instead of play up the relationship between Samantha and her new lover (Peter Finlay), a remarkably untalented film-maker.

The production, like the boat itself, is slow-paced, at least to start with. But after a landing stop near Como Park, which sees a couple of unexpected additions to the cast, the pace quickens and the laughs come more freely.

It would be unfair to reveal much more of the plot. Suffice to say that while the script is not as inventive as it might be, the trip up and down river has some nice surprises all the same.

The actors' timing cannot be faulted. Somewhere between the Morell and Swan Street bridges, for example, two of the actors were turfed overboard, complete with dinghy and a paddle. By the time the boat pulled up at Princes Walk, there they were, pedalling furiously on bicycles on the river's edge.

A lot of thought and detailed planning has gone into this enterprising venture. The result is a light and gentle entertainment with a strong sense of occasion. It should find a ready audience, as 'Storming Mont Albert' did.

On the Yarra, charting a new theatrical course

THEATRE in Melbourne has forsaken trams and buses and taken to the placid waters of the River Yarra. Theatreworks, a group of young graduates of the drama school of the Victorian College of the Arts, is the innovative company.

Last year I encountered Theatreworks for the first time on a Melbourne tram at suburban Mont Albert terminus. In 'Storming Mont Albert by Tram' we rode to the city, had an interval drink at a classy hotel, and returned to Mont Albert, diverted by a cast that was everything from the conductress to a series of passengers who boarded and left the tram at various stops. The confusion arising in the breasts of real intending passengers in the street added to our amusement, but the main source of fun was the rough situation comedy. Incidentally, the show was unrelated to the even more radical 'Bus Son of Tram', the devastatingly daft creation of the brilliant Rod Quantock.

'Storming Mont Albert by Tram' was created for Moomba but received no special funding from the festival. Its success has prompted the festival mandarins to underwrite several events in the performing arts this year, among them 'Breaking Up in Balwyn', which is a divorce party aboard the Yarra Princess. It is a splendid concept, utilising most of the main characters of 'Storming Mont Albert by Tram' whose marital and extra-marital tangles so enlivened that tram journey.

The second performance, which I saw, worked its coarse charm only after interval (spent in Como Park, Hawthorn) without ever threatening to live down to its threat of doing for divorce what 'Dimboola' did for marriage. The first act — the outward journey from Princes Walk landing — needs rewriting, which it will probably get as experience of audience reaction is gained.

The success of the earlier show on a tram was assured by the incongruity of a constant stream of

Paul Davies as Lance Tippler and Hannie Rayson as Samantha Hart-Byrne, two of the roles in 'Breaking Up in Balwyn'.

takes along Melbourne's tracks of steel. We might have been on our way to work, to a concert or a play. The essence of situation comedy was rudely shoved before us as some near-caricatures of people one sees on trams and trains (but never quite hears) suddenly revealed their turgid pseudo lives. The farther-fetched the action, the funnier it became against the background of social boredom one expects on public transport.

> **THEATRE**
> **By KEN HEALEY**

'Breaking Up in Balwyn' raises totally different expectations. We are invited to a divorce party on a riverboat, not a common, workaday form of transport. Our expectations are raised only to be dashed by boring, larger-than-life people who are teetering on the edge of the art of coarse acting.

This, by the way, is the coarseness to which I referred earlier. There is no sexual lowness in the show, and nothing to offend the most protected of great aunts.

Samantha Harte-Byrne and her boy friend, Nigel Davidson, were

ting the lunacy of the conductress and her odd passengers.

Hart-Byrne cannot, however, carry the brunt of half of a new play, even aided by her consulting psychiatrist, Dr Tamsin Smythe. Perhaps writer Paul Davies, who also raids the party as Detective Sergeant Tippler, and director Mark Shirrefs expect later audiences to become more involved in the party, helping to create their own fun by interacting with the cast. Something must be done, or some members of the public may prefer to abandon ship at Como and walk back to town in the balmy night air.

Those who make the return trip are rewarded by inanities which at least equal those of the memorable tram ride. Inventive use is made of the river, with comings and goings by various means; as interruptions to the pallid party pile one upon another, each seems funnier and more unlikely than its predecessor. In short, the show is saved.

If you visit Melbourne before April 10, inquire about the outward trip. If the word is that it has improved, then board the Yarra Princess safe in the knowledge that local theatre is charting new seas

The Herald

The Herald, Thur., Dec. 2 1982

THEATRE: Laurie Landray

Back on the track of the Mont Albert tram

ONE of the year's surprise theatrical hits, "Storming Mont Albert By Tram", presented by the Burwood-based community company Theatre Works, is to have a sequel.

Instead of an action-packed return tram trip from Mont Albert to Collins St., the audience will be invited to join Samantha Hart-Byrne on a boat trip on the Yarra to celebrate her divorce.

That will happen during next Moomba, but in the meantime Theatre Works will stage "Mary" at the Playbox Upstairs theatre from December 8-19.

The play is the result of workshops in the community for 12 months, and highlights the relationship between Australian and Greek neighbors.

SHOW SCENE

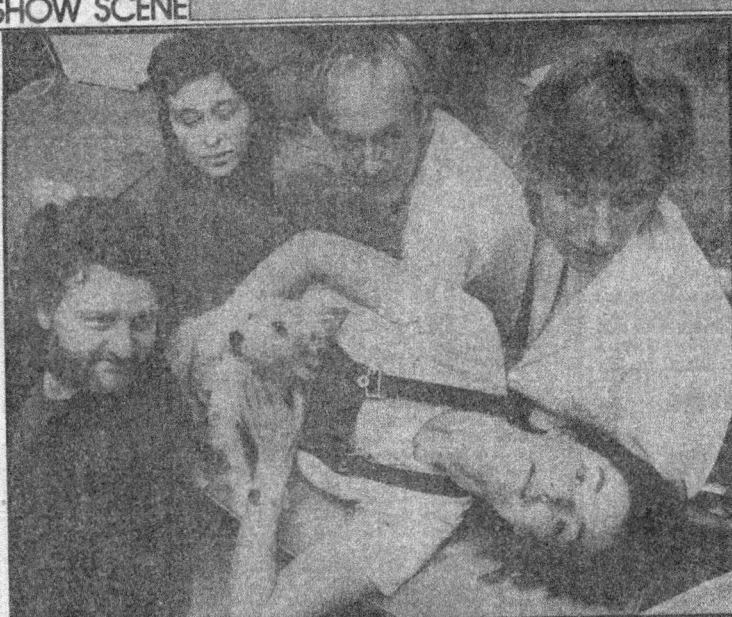

The cast of 'Breaking Up In Balwyn'.

'Tram' crew afloat

Barry Humphries will not be the only showman set afloat this Moomba. Energetic community theatre group Theatreworks, whose 'Storming Mont Albert By Tram' was such a success last year, is continuing to chronicle suburban life on the move in 'Breaking Up In Balwyn', set entirely on a Yarra riverboat.

Commuters on the Mont Albert tram will remember one Samantha Hart-Byrne, a North Balwyn socialite who was arrested with Nigel Davidson, an independent Sydney film maker with little cash flow and even less talent. After a period in the Balwyn lock-up, Nigel and Samantha were not only sharing romance but a psychiatrist, Tamsyn Smythe.

All three are reunited in 'Breaking Up In Balwyn', ostensibly Samantha's divorce party where the audience play the parts of her "very BEST friends". So horrible was Samantha's marriage that she has forgotten her wedding, so Dr Smythe has arranged the whole affair as a replica of that event, complete with cake, bells, presents and even an abominable snow-gra'n bearing salutary tidings.

Playwright Paul Davies says that his involvement of the audience in comic proceedings is one of the features of Theatreworks' ideas of community theatre.

"People feel like accomplices. In the tram show, people felt they could be hoons, too, and when it had finished, that they had shared something with other people. People would wave and say goodbye to each other."

And the subject matter, absurd though it might sound, is a reflection of the eastern suburbs community Theatreworks serves.

"This area has one of the highest divorce rates in Australia," Mr Davies says. "We have tried to focus on the economic pressures on that relationship. The real issues in the situation are never addressed and people's anger is directed through objects. We focus on the ridiculousness of it all to show that the real issues are emotional ones. Comedy is an accessible way of doing this, because we can say things you couldn't say with a more sober, tragic mode."

Like the tram in 'Storming Mont Albert', the riverboat will stop off at several jetties along the way and pause for interval and refreshments at Leonda in Hawthorn. The reception centre has been re-cast as Samantha's other's house. Apart from the not entirely unexpected visit from Senior-Sergeant Lance Tippler of the Vice, Gaming and Other Expenses Squad, the cast is anticipating a few visitors to hop aboard during the show.

Quite a few passengers unwittingly invaded the set of 'Storming Mont Albert'. Some, presumably unenthusiastic about their intended destination in the first place, would join in. Actors had to battle with other variables like the noise of the tram and the distractions of the street; on one occasion the tram was diverted around a car accident and missed the pick-up point for two of the cast, leaving the rest of the team to ad-lib valiantly until they could be found.

While cruising permits fewer disasters of this kind, mobile theatre can always include surprises. "You edit as you go along.

It's a bit like writing a film with performance timed to locations," Mr Davies says.

The performances have had to be sandwiched between other Moomba events and thus run at different times at weekends. The boat leaves the corner of Batman Avenue and Princes Bridge at 8.15 pm Tuesday to Friday, at 5 pm on weekends, and at 3 pm on March 19 and 20. During the Moomba festival, which is guaranteeing Theatreworks against loss, the boat will leave from the Morrel Bridge Landing at the corner of Anderson Street and Alexandra avenue at 3 pm.

— STEPHANIE BUNBURY

Features

A PLAY THAT CRUISES ALONG...

By ROBERT THOMSON

WHAT could be more Melbourne than a journey on the Mont Albert tram or peering over Princes Bridge at the maligned, murky Yarra?

Theatre Works, a community theatre company, last year transformed a tram into a mobile theatre for its production of "Storming Mont Albert by Tram."

Now, the Burwood-based company is to perform on the Yarra Princess riverboat.

During the return trip from Princes Bridge to Leonda, the company will present the sequel to "Storming", "Breaking up in Balwyn."

The director, Mark Shirrefs, an expatriate New South Welshman, admits to a fondness for his adopted city.

"I love Melbourne as a city. There are things you can do here that you could never do in Sydney," he said.

Mark Shirrefs believes that most people do not appreciate the significance of the Yarra.

Divides city

"The river really does divide the city in two. You only have to go along it to see the differences on each side.

"The Yarra does not have a lot of turbulence. It is a very restful thing to go down it by boat.

"We have found that the river has a calming effect on people and the action of the play acts against that."

The cast of "Breaking Up in Balwyn" get the feel of their floating theatre.

PICTURE: REY CAR

tram show was almost completely booked out."

"There were also some confused

From "SUN"
Melbourne, Vic.
4 - MAR 1983

Playground is river

MELBOURNE'S theatre is on the move—literally.

We have had plays in recent years on our trams, and even one on a travelling bus where the audience had to wear Groucho Marx glasses and noses.

Now audiences have taken to the Yarra River.

The play "Breaking Up In Balwyn" is staged on the "Yarra Princess" river boat, between Princes Bridge and Hawthorn.

Staged by Theatre Works, the play is a hilarious sequel to its production "Storming Mont Albert By Tram," a big hit with audiences and critics last year.

The play tells of North Balwyn celebrity Samantha Hart-Byrne (Hannie Rayson) and Nigel Davidson (Peter Finlay) who hire the riverboat to celebrate Samantha's divorce — with the audience guests at the party.

An interval of coffee, divorce cake and biscuits is served on one of the jetties along the river by a butler in a dress suit.

"Breaking Up In Balwyn," which is being run in conjunction with Moomba, will sail until Sunday, April 10.

It departs Tuesday to Friday at 8.15 p.m. and on weekends at 5 p.m.

Tickets are $12.90 and $6.90 for pensioners and students. Inquiries, 617-8471.

Hamming it up at rehearsals are Peter Sommerfield who plays ex-husband Michael dressed up as a Gorilla Gram and Mary Sitarenos who plays Zita Bleakville.

Play on board

BREAKING Up in Balwyn, a satire on money, marriage and divorce is being staged on board a riverboat on the Yarra.

The play is based on the short story of the same name which was awarded second prize in the City of Springvale-Syme Community Newspapers Short Story Competition.

Author Paul Davies is the resident playwright at Theatre Works who wrote last year's award winning story Storming Mont Albert By Tram which was later performed on board a moving tram.

This year's play has the same cast but this time the venue is the Yarra Princess Riverboat which will wend its way up the Yarra as events unfold.

The audience are the passengers/accomplices at a party hosted by one Samantha Hart-Byrne, a North Balwyn celebrity, after she obtains her decree nisi from Michael Hart-Byrne, a corporation lawyer and well-known tax minimiser.

The play promises to do for divorces what Dimboola did for marriages.

Among the guests you will meet as the boat makes its way up the river are Samantha and Nigel's psychiatrist. Serving you drinks will be Zeeta Bleakville, a maid with silver service experience — but how much wallop does her punch really pack? Music, dancing and films form part of the comedy nightmare river cruise.

Breaking Up in Balwyn is being performed until Sunday 10 April and the boat leaves from Princess Walk Landing, corner Batman Ave. and Princes Bridge every weeknight at 8.15 pm.

On weekends it will leave from Princes Walk Landing at 5 pm except for 19, 20 March when it will leave at 3 pm.

The Moomba holiday weekend, 12, 13 March, the boat will leave from Morrell Bridge Landing, corner Anderson St. and Alexandra Ave., South Yarra at 3 pm.

Tickets cost $12.90 for adults with a $6.90 concession ticket available for pensioners, students and unemployed and are avail-

A riot of a show!

IT promises to be a riot!

Our local theatre group, Theatre Works, has devised a sequel to the amazing 'Storming Mont Albert By tram', last year's Moomba hit.

This time the same cast are going to board a boat at the Princes Walk landing, sail up the Yarra and talk about money, marriage and divorce, in a wonderful extravaganza entitled 'Breaking Up in Balwyn'.

The story revolves around Samantha Hart-Byrne, a young Balwyn lady celebrating her divorce from husband Michael, corporation lawyer and well known tax minimiser.

Don't miss this unique trip. The boat departs weekends and weekdays. Bookings are available at Bass outlets.

Here's to a long and happy life ... Michael Hart-Byrne disgui Samantha's (left) party while maid Zeeta Bleak

"MOUNTAIN DISTRICT FREE PRESS" Vic.

16 FEB 1983

6 — THE FREE PRESS, Wednesday, 16 February 1983.

Chief of police of the Vice, Gaming and Other Expenses Squad Lance Tipler handcuffs Mrs Hart-Byrne in the midd[le] of the boat party.

Dr Tainsin Smythe, psychiatrist, hydrothe[ra]pist and beautician puts in his tuppence wo[rth] as Samantha and her new boyfriend Nigel ha[...]

All aboard for a rage on the river

A RIVERBOAT is the stage for a new play called Breaking Up In Balwyn.

Theatre Works is presenting the play on the riverboat that cruises up the Yarra River, in the heart of Melbourne.

Breaking Up In Balwyn takes the form of a party hosted by Samantha (Hannie Rayson) to celebrate her divorce from Michael (Peter Sommerfeld).

Samantha hires the riverboat for the occasion, and involves the passengers in events as the boat makes its way up the Yarra from Princess Bridge to Como Park and back.

There's music, dancing, a film show, and a visit from the vice squad.

Playwright Paul Davies is an incorrigible river boat traveller and is the resident writer for Theatre Works, this year.

The play runs from February 24 to April 10, and departs from the Princes Walk Landing.

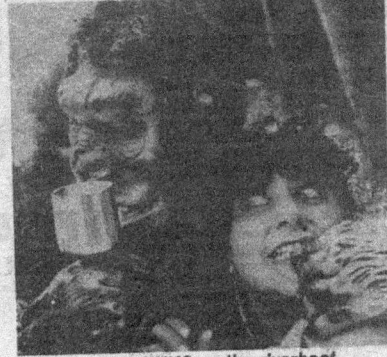

★ HI-JINKS on the riverboat.

THEATRE: Laurie Landray

Back on the track of the Mont Albert tram

ONE of the year's surprise theatrical hits, "Storming Mont Albert By Tram", presented by the Burwood-based community company Theatre Works, is to have a sequel.

Instead of an action-packed return tram trip from Mont Albert to Collins St., the audience will be invited to join Samantha Hart-Byrne on a boat trip on the Yarra to celebrate her divorce.

That will happen during next Moomba, but in the meantime Theatre Works will stage "Mary" at the Playbox Upstairs theatre from December 8-19.

The play is the result of workshops in the community for 12 months, and highlights the relationship between Australian and Greek neighbors.

☐ ☐ ☐ ☐ ☐ ☐

Contemporary Dance Theatre, comprising 15 dancers from the Victorian College of Arts, will present "New Feats and Faces 2", a project designed to give creative opportunities to young choreographers, from tonight until Saturday at the Open Stage, corner of Grattan and Swanston Sts., Carlton.

Peter Matthews is artistic director, and other choreographers taking part include Wayne Bacon, Julie Anne Long, Penelope Nunn and John Utans.

Dance lecturer Jan Stripling, formerly of the Stuttgart Ballet, is also assisting.

☐ ☐ ☐ ☐ ☐ ☐

Space did not permit me to comment on Margaret Wilson's excellent new ballet, "Frieze", in my review of the Australian Dance Theatre's current program at the Princess.

It created a taut mood of icy wastes peopled by hunters and hunted, with a finely characterised hunted deer by Victoria Jestyn.

Modern dance lovers on the dole couldn't do better than take advantage of the $5 tickets offered to the unemployed for this show.

☐ ☐ ☐ ☐ ☐ ☐

Tom Rothfield, who was recently back in Australia from Europe to stage his play "Chekhov in Love", reckons his drama "Jam Tomorrow" was the first Australian play to be seen in London when it went on at the Torch Theatre in 1939.

But it has never made the limelight in Australia, because the actors walked off the job when it was in rehearsal at the Little Theatre, South Yarra.

They were protesting at dialogue between Australian farmers and English settlers — and you can discover why, and note the chasm between Rothfield's drama and Harry Reade's "The Naked Gun" (now being played at Athenaeum 2) if you compare the scripts, both just published by Yackandandah Playscripts.

Theatre is the liveliest art, and drama can be a significant tool for social change, personal growth and the exploration of society and relationships. According to choice it can reinforce or challenge the prevailing values. It is a political process: by making theatre, members of a community can make statements about their lives. By making theatre we can entertain, educate, explore, explain.

Theatre can also be, and too often is, boring deadly, uninteresting, irrelevant, unchallenging and unilluminating. For that reason we have no 'mass' audience for a diverse and lively contemporary theatre. There is no tradition of wide public support for a challenging and relevant national drama.

". . a radical theatre. . "

Instead, we are fed a diet of the safe and the comfortable. By entrepreneurs, advertising, television and the 'star' system who conspire to present the predictable, the spineless, 'nice', the offensive. Without a dynamic alternative, audiences will remain uncritical consumers of such bland fare. In the early seventies playwright, Jack Hibberd called for (roughly) a hard theatre, a radical theatre, a larrikan theatre. Over a decade later such a call is still relevant. It is precisely those qualities that seven years of conservative government and recession have nearly starved out the arts and education.

'The Yartz' now face severe restrictions, and restraint is felt across the board. The Victorian Government seems set to announce a 4½% cut in arts funding that could well prove disastrous for a range of performing arts organisations. While experimental companies are collapsing around the country, big business musicals boom along in Sydney and Melbourne.

'Breaking Up In Balwyn'

Melbourne at the moment supports a vital and exciting alternative theatre scene. Community based companies like Theatreworks and West perform original work that reflects the lives and aspirations of their host communities. Plays like 'Breaking Up In Balwyn' performed on a Yarra Cruise boat, and 'Mary' — growing up in an Italian migrant family — feed directly into a stream of truly indigenous theatre.

". decorative dinos[aurs]

By contrast, decorative dinos[aurs] the Australian Ballet and the A[ustralian] Opera continue to siphon [large] amounts of 'arts money' fro[m] Federal coffers and industry fou[ndations].

The work of these companies [may be] excellent, and without doub[t give] a great deal of pleasure to thou[sands of] people. Yet I wonder what [could be] achieved in terms of contempor[ary] or local and relevant work if thes[e] giant[s] did not so uncritically [absorb] huge amounts of very limited [funds].

Tony MacGregor

Lot's Wife is published by the Publications Committee, on behalf of the Monash Association of Students.

8—TRUTH, SATURDAY, FEB. 19, 1983

Breaking Up — it's all aboard!

A RIVERBOAT is the stage for a new play called Breaking Up in Balwyn.

Theatre Works is presenting the play on the riverboat that cruises up the Yarra River, in the heart of Melbourne.

Breaking Up in Balwyn takes the form of a party hosted by Samantha (Hannie Rayson) to celebrate her divorce from Michael (Peter Sommerfeld).

Samantha hires the riverboat for the occasion, and involves the passengers in events as it cruises from Princess Bridge to Como Park and back.

There's music, dancing, a film show, and a visit from the vice squad.

Playwright Paul Davies is an incurable river boat traveller and this year's resident writer for Theatre Works.

The play runs from February 24 to April 10, and the boat leaves from the Princes Walk Landing.

SUBURBIA · DISINTEGRATES
·AN ANATOMY OF BALWYN·

There's something about Balwyn.
Toorak shares its affluence, but lacks its overpowering conformity.
Hawthorn has a similar comfortable respectability, but doesn't even approach Balwyn for sheer tacky *newness*. Bulleen has the same upper-middle-class pretentions, but loses out on architectural restraint (read "brick veneer").
Even Dandenong shares Balwyn's cultural blankness
but lacks its BMW's.
No other Melbourne suburb is so utterly bereft of
squalor, poverty, bohemians and imagination.
Nowhwere else could you see, at eight-thirty in the morning,
a dressing-gowned figure hosing down the front concrete — in the rain.
That's Balwyn.
Even its name: "Bal-wyn" — it sounds as if some advertising executive made the word up yesterday, to *sound* as if it had a respectable history.
No other Melbourne suburb so completely epitomises the foibles of upper-middle-class Australia. Consequently, no other suburb is quite so vulnerable to the jabs of satire, spoof and send-up.

Paul Davies "Breaking Up in Balwyn" is the latest comedy to jump on the Balwyn-baiting bandwagon. Or rather, not quite the bandwagon: the play is performed on a boat, the Yarra Princess, during its cruise up the Yarra and back.

This Theatre Works production is a sequel to the very successful "Storming Mont Albert by Tram". Three of the characters are common to both plays: "independent Sydney film-maker" Nigel Davidson (Peter Finlay), his new lover and Balwyn socialite — Samantha Hart-Byrne (Hanny Rayson); and Nigel's ex-lover Cathy Waterman (Caz Howard) who appears as a policeperson from the Vice-Gaming and Other Expenses Squad (Mounted).

The setting this time is Samantha's "divorce party", the night after she has sundered the marital ties with her ex, Michael (who appears later in the show

From "MELBOURNE TIMES" City & Suburbs
16 MAR 1983

Cinema : Dance : Theatre

Good natured satire adrift

BREAKING UP IN BALWYN
On the Yarra

Theatre

By J. ELLISON

Theatre Works is a welcome alternative to some of the more conservative, commercial groups. *Breaking Up in Balwyn* is real theatre; certainly theatrical in the best sense of the word.

From the moment you line up at Princes Walk waiting to board the Yarra Princess, there is a sense of excitement, celebration and fun.

Samantha Hart-Byrne has invited guests (the audience) to celebrate her divorce from the rather disreputable Michael Hart-Byrne (race track identity and tax minimiser).

Also aboard are Samantha's latest love Nigel Davidson (independent Sydney film-maker) and Dr Tamsin Smythe (consulting psychiatrist, hydro-therapist and beautician) who is attempting to ensure a smooth transition for Samantha from the bonds of matrimony to the freedom of being a swinging single.

Samantha has also hired a French maid for the occasion, but all the French maids are out — so she gets Lerlene Fowler instead.

The trip is traumatic, to say the least, for Samantha and her cronies but for the "guests" it is hilarious.

The script works on gags and general send ups of cliched images of characters we all know so well. But it is good-natured satire, qualitatively different to the sourness of, say, Edna Everage humour.

There is certainly never a dull moment. Though the logistics of managing a play like this present some problems with timing, the pace is generally cracking.

However, we do get to see one too many of Nigel's films, which, though they add to the plot in a minor way do slow the zestful action.

The environment doesn't overwhelm the action (which is not confined to the boat) and adds to the great theatricality which characterises the show.

Breaking Up In Balwyn is an inspired sequel to *Storming Mont Albert By Tram* and should meet with equal success. The question is: Where will the next play be?

THE AGE

Thursday 10 February 1983 — *Arts*

Paul Davies (left) and Mark Shirrefs: getting ready to storm Leonda by riverboat.

Pioneers jump from tram to boat

INTERVIEW
Mary-Louise O'Callaghan

IN THE DIM interior of the old Canterbury Library a long string has been tied across the room about two metres above the floor.

It is an integral part of the rehearsals for Theatre Work's latest production, 'Breaking up in Balwyn'. It is there to acclimatise the cast to the low ceiling in the riverboat, The Yarra Princess, where they will be performing the show.

On the Yarra from 24 February, 'Breaking up in Balwyn' comes after the group's success last year with 'Storming Mont Albert by Tram', Melbourne's first play to be performed on a tram.

A river party to celebrate socialite Samantha Hart-Byrne's divorce, the production uses many of the characters and cast from 'Storming Mont Albert by Tram' and is being directed by the same director, Mark Shirrefs.

"'Balwyn' is a much more complicated piece of theatre; the characters are the same as 'Tram' but they are a lot more developed," Mark Shirrefs says. "In 'Tram' there was opportunity to play with how people relate to each other in a chance encounter after not seeing each other for some time. In 'Balwyn' we are able to develop this further.

"Technically too, it is a lot more involved. We are going to use some film or video during the show to explain some of the relationships and to give some of the background detail, so we don't have to use the dialogue for that."

Paul Davies is the official creator of the play and its predecessor but he stresses that the development of both scripts have been a collective effort. He is the 1983 writer-in-residence at Theatre Works and began working on the script after winning the Syme-Springvale City Short Story Competition last year with a prose version of the river party.

"We then spent about four weeks together developing the script," he says. "I recorded those discussions and really became the person who went away and typed up everybody's ideas. Quite a few members of the group have written their own plays so the distinction between writer and cast is deliberately blurred. The actors have to be able to improvise because the nature of the play invites unforeseen circumstances. They really develop the script on the spot."

Davies used a trip to Brisbane to finish the script and also to film the "anti-honeymoon" of Samantha and her new love, Nigel, at Noosa.

"Noosa is such a Victorian creation. I thought it would be rather appropriate for Nigel and Samantha," Davies says. "And we're able to bring it into the show through video along with film of Samantha's first wedding and some of the footage of last year's 'Tram'."

For interval, the show will moor at Leonda, which becomes the home of Samantha's mother. "There is a parallel with 'Apocalypse Now' in that, I suppose," Shirrefs jokes. "The journey up the river to the womb and back down again.

"'Tram's was a straight farce whereas 'Balwyn' is much more complicated and we have scope to deal a bit more with some issues. Paul, having been through a divorce himself, has been able to point a finger at some of the issues that divorce involves. But all in a very light-hearted way.

"The whole thing of the way the Yarra divides the city into poor areas and South of The Yarra really is a metaphor for the play in lots of ways and is something that it deals with," he says.

"I think shows like 'Tram' and 'Balwyn', just because of their curiosity value, bring people to the theatre who don't normally go," he said.

"Once you get out of the theatre into an environment that isn't controlled, a performance gets a roughness, a life that you just don't get in a more formal atmosphere. Night-to-night the actors have to cope with a different set of circumstances and have to concentrate on improvising with whatever happens."

Breaking Up will break you up

by DEIRDRE BLACK

THEATRE always tries to make each night a little different to try to create a certain freshness, but with Breaking Up in Balwyn, not even the actors and actresses can anticipate what will happen.

Breaking Up in Balwyn is being performed on a ferry travelling up the Yarra to Leonda and back.

The Theatre Works cast, though, is not unfamiliar with this style of theatre.

Last year, the group produced Storming Mont Albert by Tram on a tram and caused laughter all along the tracks from Mont Albert terminus to the city and back.

Paul Davies, resident writer at Theatre Works and writer of Tram and Breaking Up in Balwyn, said there would be some interaction with the public in the new show.

The play starts during Moomba and the ferry will be travelling through water ski program and Henley on Regatta events.

Breaking Up in Balwyn is the sequel to Tram and most of that cast will appear in a more developed form in this play.

Samantha the social butterfly will be the main focus for the play. Since meeting Nigel, the trendy filmmaker from Sydney, Samantha has decided to divorce her husband. Nigel and Samantha met during the last play in jail.

To celebrate her divorce, Samantha is holding a party on the ferry with all her friends.

At the same time, Samantha has slight amnesia which causes her to lose all memory of her marriage to Michael.

By coincidence, Samantha shares the same psychiatrist with her new boyfriend Nigel, but that is not all Nigel and Samantha share.

While they were in the 'clink,' Nigel had decided they had a lot to share — her money and his talent.

Anyway, the psychiatrist, Dr Tamsin Smythe, decides to set the party up like Samantha's wedding in the hope that her memory will be jogged.

Naturally, in a play like this Samantha's ex-husband and Nigel's ex-girlfriend Cathy turn up.

Although Paul Davies expects Breaking Up to play to packed houses, he does not expect a profit to be made.

The play uses an unusual venue, and as a result the fewer seats available forces Theatre Works to rely on grants and subsidies to break even.

He said he had received money from the Literary Board and the Victorian Ministry of the Arts.

THE maid (left) eavesdrops on a conversation between divorced husband Michael (in the gorilla suit) and psychiatrist Dr Tamsin.

Breaking up the crowds

Works presented 'Storming Mont Albert by Tram', a zany look at trams and their passengers, set on a moving tram.

Originally scheduled for 16 sessions, 'Tram' was an off-the-rail success, playing to packed Number 42 Specials for over 80 performances.

Well, this Moomba, this imaginative community theatre company is launching a sequel to 'Tram', "launching" being the vital word. It's set on the Yarra Princess — a river cruise boat.

Once again, Theatre Works has injected a liberal dose of satire into life in the eastern suburbs, where the group is based.

'Breaking up in Balwyn' — "a toast to money, marriage and divorce" — retains some of the 'Tram' characters and introduces many new, crazy ones. 'Tram's' director, Mark Shirrefs, and writer, Paul Davies, are again at the helm with 'Balwyn'.

"The idea for this show sort of grew organically out of the 'Tram' show," Paul Davies told Weekender recently.

"The link is trendy Balwyn housewife Samantha Hart-Byrne, played by Hannie Rayson. On the 'Tram', Sam was on her way to an MTC play, but during the course of the evening she has a few too many and on her tram ride home she is tipsy enough to start inviting everyone back to her celebratory bash for her impending divorce — sort of a marriage wake — and, as with the 'Tram' show, the audience/passengers are an active part of the action.

Paul Davies thinks such bizarre venues as trams and riverboats make for greater intimacy with audiences. A full house on the tram was 50. With the boat it will be 80.

"An interesting relationship is built with the audience," he said. "There's no division, no barriers. It's like a sophisticated form of street theatre.

"No, it's closer to film making, I think. When you shoot a scene on location — in a street, let's say — the real, day-to-day world is a backdrop to the scripted action. Most theatre takes place in a dark venue. It is set in unreality."

It can also be said that Theatre Works enjoys a captive audience. Late-comers won't — or can't — be admitted and people who don't like the show can't get up and walk out.

'Breaking up in Balwyn' runs for two hours — an hour upriver to Leonda Park and then all the way back after interval. The script has to be timed precisely to allow for the entrances and exits characters make from the landings en route, just as the 'Tram' characters used the tram stops.

In 'Tram', the actors sometimes were

Riot of a comedy set on the Yarra

BREAKING Up in Balwyn, a satire on money, marriage and divorce takes place on board a riverboat on the Yarra.

The play is based on the short story of the same name which was awarded second prize in the City of Springvale-Syme Community Newspapers Short Story Competition.

Author Paul Davies is the resident playwright at Theatre Works who wrote last year's award winning story Storming Mont Albert By Tram which was later performed on board a moving tram.

This year's play has the same cast but this time the venue is the Yarra Princess Riverboat which will wind its way up the Yarra as events unfold.

The audience are the passengers/accomplices at a party hosted by one Samantha Hart-Byrne, a North Balwyn celebrity, after she obtains her decree nisi from Michael Hart-Byrne, a corporation lawyer and well-known tax-minimiser.

The play promises to do for divorces what Dimboola did for marriages.

Among the guests you will meet as the boat makes its way up river are Samantha and Nigel's psychiatrist. Serving you drinks will be Zeeta Bleakville, a maid with silver service experience — but how much wallop does her punch really pack?

Music, dancing and films form part of the comedy nightmare river cruise.

Breaking Up in Balwyn will be performed from Thursday 24 February to Sunday 10 April and the boat leaves from Princess Walk Landing, corner Batman Ave., and Princes Bridge every weeknight at 8.15 pm.

On weekends it will leave from Princes Walk Landing at 5 pm except for 19, 20 March when it will leave at 3 pm.

On Special Moomba weekends 5, 6, 12, 13 March the boat will leave from Morrell Bridge Landing, corner Anderson St., and Alexandra Ave., South Yarra at 3 pm.

Tickets cost $12.90 for adults with a $6.90 concession ticket available for pensioners, students and unemployed and are available at all Bass outlets.

Hamming it up at rehearsals last week are from left Hamie Rayson who plays Samantha Hart-Byrne, Peter Somerfeld who plays ex-husband Michael all done up as a Gorilla Gram and Mary Sitarenos who plays Zita Bleakville.

Theatre on the river

THEATRE Works, the Eastern suburbs community theatre company, will open its new play later this month on the Yarra Princess river boat.

The company will present Breaking Up In Balwyn, a Paul Davies satire on money, marriage and divorce, from Thursday, February 24 to Sunday, April 10.

The play is directed by mark Shirrefs and stars the seven members of Theatre Works.

The company was formed in 1981 and works from Burwood's Victoria College. As well as presenting plays it runs community workshops.

Yarra Princess will leave from Princes Walk landing, corner Batman Avenue and Prices Bridge, for all regular performances.

The boat will leave at 8.15 pm from Tuesday to Friday and at 5 pm at weekends (March 19 and 20 at 3 pm). During Moomba weekends, March 5 and 6 and 12 and 13, Yarra Princess will leave from Morrell Bridge landing (corner Anderson St and Alexander Ave, South Yarra). All trips will be to Como Park and return.

Tickets are $12.90 for adults and $6.90 concession. Bookings at Bass outlets. For more information ring Theatre Works on 285 0287.

TOORAK TIMES

the paper for the socially a...

29/3/1...

Juicy Titbits with JAN THOMPSON

★★★

TAKE a gorilla, divorcee, lover, ex-husband, ex girlfriend, two police officers a "mental as anything" maid who looked like an escapee from "One Flew Over The Cuckoos Nest", life jacket and life boat, coffee and wedding cake up some dark ramp in Burnley and what have you got? A divorce party called "They're Breaking up in Balwyn".

We boarded the "Sea Princess" at Princess Pier to be guests of a divorce party which was held cruising down the Yarra. Indeed, the experience was most novel and although Theatre Works company obviously rehearsed and rehearsed laboriously, I for one was up the creek with this play. To mind mind, it was over acted and non professional, although my friends enjoyed it from woe to go, which just goes to prove you must see it yourself to form an opinion. Perhaps had there been a little Vodka mixed with the orange juice, we would have loosened up and voted it a winner. Who knows?

★★★

PAGE 8 — PEOPLE... ISSUES...

"THE SUN" 2/2/83

MOOMBA

By GRAEME JOHNSTONE

Sir Leslie

...goes for the 'Yartz'

NCY doing a bit of "time"? You ow, Porridge. In a dank cell in Old Melbourne Jail.

u can try it at Moomba year.
the play "Hard Labor, ", the audience gets ed up. The door clangs , and in the eerie light re surrounded by the h masks of former in- es, including Ned Kelly. ter you are let out to see est of the play — but only you've been in there enough "to get the feel- as Moomba manager Moors says.
ard Labor, Mate" is g presented by the West atre at the request of mba management — and art of a stronger arts ponent being added to bourne's festival of fun. ertainly, the traditional gs are there for Melb- e's 29th Moomba, which from February 27 to ch 14.

★★

e King, who will be ounced today, will, as l, rule over the carnival, water-skiing, the music, grand parade, and so on. t this year sees an im- ement in theatre, writing concert performances. ese range from plays, to turies-old Japanese ic, to modern jazz-rock. ppropriately a star perfor- is Doctor Sir Leslie Colin erson, Australia's cham- t of "the Yartz."
e have been closely look- at where the festival ld be going," said Mr rs.
e have a very strong lic community base — a with events that th lic readily identifies wit he water-skiing, the carn , music shows and so on. nd we will make them ter each year.
ut we sat down and d ourselves: 'What aren't doing?'

"We find that it's mainly in the area of drama, dance and literature that we haven't been putting in enough work."
Mr Moors says that Moomba will now appeal to this section with "stunning re- sults."

Other plays requested inc- lude, "Secrets", by the Hand- span Puppet Theatre, and "Breaking Up In Balwyn" by Theatre Works, the producers of last year's successful "Stor- ming Mont Albert by Tram."
"Breaking Up" examines a collapsing eastern suburbs marriage — and it all hap- pens on a Yarra river-boat.
"Latecomers," Mr Moors warns, "cannot be admitted."
Mr Moors sees this concept as "exciting" and "in line with creating opportunities for creative people."
"We asked the three comp- anies to come up with some- thing special," he said.

★★★★

"We are endevoring to give Melbourne and Victorian artists in all spheres — music, drama, dance and literature — the opportunity to do something special at festival time," said Mr Moors.
Does he see this as a matur- ing of Moomba?
"I think so," he said. "Whether it will be eventually the Melbourne Moomba Arts Festival — with that word added in there — is another matter."

But he does not see it as an Adelaide Arts Festival.
"No, I don't think that is totally necessary in Melb- ourne," he said. "We have an enormous amount of arts events in Melbourne during the year.
"Adelaide, on the other hand, has less chance to see shows that are put on in Melbourne and Sydney.
"Thus, they need it. But I don't mean that in a deroga- tory sense.
"Moomba is bigger than that. It's the biggest single festival in Australia."
Two million people use the Alexandra Gardens during Moomba, and more than 500,000 watch the parade.
"When you get those sorts of crowds, you know you have an event that's working.
"And our aim is to improve and add to it."

BREAKING UP IN BALWYN

A satire on marriage, money and divorce, but not necessarily in that order. Written and performed for the Festival by **Theatre Works** and staged on board the **Yarra Princess**, Melbourne's "Love Boat" cruising the **Yarra River**.

A sequel to last year's Moomba hit **"Storming Mont Albert by Tram"**. Now Theatre Works goes off the rails and into the river! Join North Balwyn celebrity **Samantha Hart-Byrne** and her new boyfriend **Nigel Davidson** (independent Sydney film maker) for the party of your lives. A madcap, boat-ride play with films, music, dancing and light refreshments.

Please note that latecomers cannot be admitted.

Season commences **Thursday Feb 24 to Sunday April 10**. Boat departs Princes Walk Landing (Cnr Batman Ave and Princes Bridge) weekdays —Tuesday to Friday at **8.15 pm**. Weekends 5 pm. special **Moomba weekends** March 5, 6, 12, 13, 19 and 20 departing Morell Bridge Landing (Cnr Anderson Street and Alexandra Ave South Yarra) at **3 pm**.

Tickets: Adults $12.90. Concession $6.90.

Bookings at all BASS outlets. Inquiries Theatre Works 285 0287.

The West Theatre Company, Theatre Works and Handspan Theatre Ltd, acknowledge the assistance of the Theatre Board of the Australia Council, a statutory body of the Commonwealth Government, and the Victorian Ministry for the Arts.

The Australian Playwrights Theatre presents:—

THE DOMINATOR
by Ray Mooney

The Dominator is a survivor in a brutal world in which no-one is protected. For the Dominator, the king-hit is the answer to life's little problems, and to have one mate for him is to have one weakness too many.

AN AUTOBIOGRAPHY OF AN EXTRA
by Judith Ferrier and Ray Mooney

It is a non-naturalistic play about the highs and lows of an actress destined to be a permanent extra. The work is structured to resemble a real-life soapie or B-Grade movie, in which the extra's imagined reality provides the rationalization for her motivation.

Both plays at **La Mama**, 205 Faraday Street, Carlton from Wednesday **Mar 2** to Sunday **Mar 13** (Wednesday to Sunday) at **8 pm**.

Tickets: Adults $6, Concessions $3.50.

Bookings at Readings Bookshop 347 6085.

DR D
by Kris Hemensley

The life and times of Celine cast as a Punch and Judy Show.

This play poses many questions. attempts answers to none . . .

If you are confused before you see it you may not mind quite so much once you have.

Playing at the **Gala Room**, City Square from Monday **Mar 2** to Monday **Mar 14** (No sunday performances) at **7.30 pm**.

Tickets: Adults $6, Concessions $3.50. Available at Door.

POETRY AND PLAY READINGS

The **Melbourne Artists Festival** will present a daily programme of **Poetry and Play** readings and workshops from **Feb 28** to **Mar 14**.

The venue is the **City Square**. Readings in the Gala Room 10 am to 6 pm, Small Publishers Book Fair in the Information Centre 10 am to 5 pm, Performance Poetry in the Amphitheatre 10 am to 5 pm. The Melbourne Poetry Society presents prize winning and published poets and work of promising new poets. Programme will include musical presentations. Thursday Mar 3, 2 to 4 pm.

review:

Breaking Up in Balwyn,
The Yarra Princess Riverboat,
Princes Walk Landing.

It is an audience's prerogative to leave a play at any stage of a performance. Unless you are a good swimmer or don't mind getting wet, it is almost impossible to leave midway through a performance of Breaking Up in Balwyn.

The whole play is presented onboard the Yarra Princess riverboat which cruises up the Yarra River to Como landing and back. Luckily the play is entertaining enough to hold audience interest. No-one appeared prepared to jump off the boat and head for shore the night I saw the production.

Breaking Up in Balwyn is presented by Theatre Works which last year staged the highly successful Storming Mont Albert by Tram. The audience attending that production could at least pull the cord and alight from the tram if desired.

But there are no second chances once onboard the Yarra Princess. This play is a daunting experience. The moment one boards the riverboat you become an invited guest of Samantha Hart-Byrne's divorce party.

Initially the aspiring upper-class Samantha (played by Hannie Rayson) is all smiles. She is accompanied by her new friend, a novice independent Sydney film maker called Nigel (Peter Finlay) and her personal therapist, Dr Tamsin Smythe (Susie Fraser).

The party gets off to a flying start as the boat heads for Como landing. The audience toasts Samantha's new found freedom and are also treated to a preview of Nigel's latest film on video screens at each end of the boat.

However, ominous signs appear that not all is well. A dark-haired pretty woman consistently pops up in Nigel's film to Samantha's disgust and all Nigel's presents are cans of deodorant. Then suddenly Samantha has a seizure when reminded of her first wedding.

The proceedings return to relative normality when a Gorilla-Gram arrives via a quick stop halfway up river. The fireworks begin again when it turns out to be ex-husband Michael Hart-Byrne (Peter Sommerfeld).

The storyline is rather silly and the characters blatantly stereotyped.

However, a mixture of the novelty of being onboard the riverboat, funny throw-away one-liners and a feeling of being part of the action, makes the play work.

Mary Sitarenos' character, Lerlene, is also a savior. At times she is left on landings while the boat cruises on and she is even cast adrift in a rubber dinghy. From the outset she talks to the audience and puts them beyond the proscenium arch.

It is the unusual side of the play that makes it entertaining. Without all the frills Paul Davies' play could not stand alone. Ten marks to Theatre Works for attempting a production like this. It is certainly innovative theatre. — **Robert Gibson.**

this week in MELBOURNE
A guide to the best in Melbourne
No. 1245 March 25-March 31, 1983

BREAKING UP IN BALWYN
The Yarra Princess Riverboat (departs Princess Walk Landing – cnr Batman Avenue and Princes Bridge. Written by Paul Davies and directed by Mark Shirrefs. The play is a satire on money, marriage and divorce but not necessarily in that order. Stars Paul Davies, Peter Finlay, Susie Fraser, Caz Howard, Mary Sitarenos, Peter Sommerfield and Hannie Rayson. Departs at 8.15pm Tuesday to Friday and 5pm weekends. Special Moomba weekend performances March 5, 6, 12 and 13 – departs from Morrell Bridge Landing – cnr Alexandra Avenue and Anderson Street. Season until April 10. Presented by Theatre Works.

The break up — on a boat

IT'S "open house" to an exclusive party to be held on a ferry cruising the Yarra.

But it's a party of a difference — you'll watch Theatre Works creating a party for your amusement and learn about the lives of North Balwyn society.

Breaking Up In Balwyn is the name of the group's satiric production which makes you chuckle and think about the trials of money, marriage and divorce.

Last year for Moomba the group presented Storming Mont Albert by Tram, which attracted a lot of interest.

Many people thought it was just an ordinary tram and got quite a surprise when they boarded it and discovered they had stepped into the middle of an unfolding drama.

The ferry will be the novel situation of another creative play performed by the cast.

Theatre Works is assisted by the Theatre Board of the Australia Council and the Victorian Ministry for the Arts.

The show begins on Thursday, February 24 and goes until April 10.

It will be held on the Yarra Princess Riverboat which departs (with or without you) at 8.15 p.m. from Tuesday to Friday, from the Princes Walk landing, cnr. Batman Av. and Princes Bridge.

On weekends the riverboat leaves at 5 p.m.

On March 5, 6, 12 and 13 — special Moomba weekends — it will leave from the Morrell Bridge landing, cnr. Anderson St. and Alexandra Av., South Yarra.

Bookings are available through Bass and for any inquiries ring 617-8471.

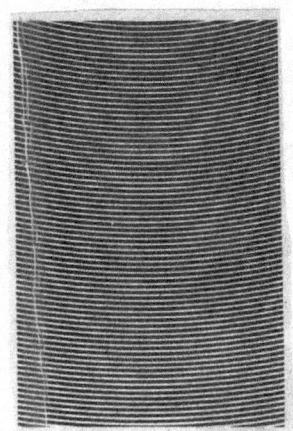

THE STUDENTS' NEWSMAGAZINE

Farrago, Volume 61, 11th March, 1983

Paul Davies "Breaking Up in Balwyn" is the latest comedy to jump on the Balwyn-baiting bandwagon. Or rather, not quite the bandwagon: the play is performed on a boat, the Yarra Princess, during its cruise up the Yarra and back.

This Theatre Works production is a sequel to the very successful "Storming Mont Albert by Tram". Three of the characters are common to both plays: "independent Sydney film-maker" Nigel Davidson (Peter Finlay), his new lover and Balwyn socialite — Samantha Hart-Byrne (Hanny Rayson); and Nigel's ex-lover Cathy Waterman (Caz Howard) who appears as a policeperson from the Vice-Gaming and Other Expenses Squad (Mounted).

The setting this time is Samantha's "divorce party", the night after she has sundered the marital ties with her ex, Michael (who appears later in the show dressed initially in a gorilla suit!) The audience who are encouraged to participate, are supposed to be Samantha's guests at the maritime party, and she makes a great show of cheek-pecking and familiar greetings.

The cast is completed by Lerlene Fowler (Mary Sitarenos), a working-class waitress; tax minimizer Michael Hart-Byrne (Peter Somerfield); Sergeant Lance Tippler (author Paul Davies); and psychiatrist Dr. Tamsin Smythe (Susie Fraser) who constantly consoles the other characters with soothing psychobabble.

The farcical action revolves entirely around the silly pretentions of the middle-class, with occasional doses of caustic *common*-sense from Lerlene.

If you think this is rather thin material for a play, you're right; but fortunately there's more to this play than plot. There's plenty to watch; characters arrive by rowboat or are picked up from the shore, the cast is continually called upon to improvise so that the boat and the story are both in the right places. The events are so unexpected that they often take the actors by surprise. It relies entirely on novelty value — and what's wrong with that?

But is "Breaking Up in Balwyn" just another example of "the middle-class entertaining themselves"? How much of the laughter is of sympathy and recognition?

Director Mark Shireffs: "There's no predominant group, the audience seems to come from all over the place. It certainly attracts a lot of people who wouldn't go to ordinary theatre because of the novelty value.

But it is probably true that there's an element of recognition in the laughter. We've set out to portray certain archetypes: the trendy film-maker, the socialite, the tax-evading businessman — the whole upper-middle-class way of doing things because they're "novel" then paying a psychiatrist afterwards to tell them that it was alright to do it, that it wasn't "sick" — all the silly things you can do when you've got money: your life is based on the assumption that if something's wrong then you pay to have it fixed up.

"All the characters are pretty neurotic — I hesitate to say completely fucked — but all of them want something from Samantha. She's an unfortunate victim, her problem seems to be a common one, especially among upper-middle-class people who have money and aren't ever called upon to make any real choices in their own lives; they're at the mercy of those who have a bit more shrewdness or cunning".

"Breaking Up" has a very "theatre restaurant" kind of flavour about it. Says Shireffs:

"Theatre restaurants are no longer "alternative" they've become pretty established now. A lot of our audience are the people who are now going to the Last Laugh.

Melbourne audiences are more receptive to something a bit bizzarre. Sydney theatre leans toward extravagant productions. In Melbourne they go for content rather than style, so more novel things are done here — for example "Bus, Son of Tram' ".

Moomba's river festivities will cause all sorts of problems for the show, but Mark doesn't mind.

It's good that Moomba is supporting us they've never supported theatre before. It's always been so sport oriented, and its good to see other possibilities being opened up, different ideas and different people coming out. Adelaide and Sydney have their Arts Festivals; and it's good that Moomba is developing this way because its the closest thing Melbourne's got".

HERALD features

The Herald, Wed., March 2, 1983

By ROBERT THOMSON

WHAT could be more Melbourne than a journey on the Mont Albert tram or peering over Princes Bridge at the maligned, murky Yarra?

Theatre Works, a community theatre company, last year transformed a tram into a mobile theatre for its production of "Storming Mont Albert by Tram."

Now, the Burwood-based company is to perform on the Yarra Princess riverboat.

During the return trip from Princes Bridge to Leonda, the company will present the sequel to "Storming", "Breaking up in Balwyn."

The director, Mark Shirrefs, an expatriate New South Welshman, admits to a fondness for his adopted city.

"I love Melbourne as a city. There are things you can do here that you could never do in Sydney," he said.

Mark Shirrefs believes that most people do not appreciate the significance of the Yarra.

Divides city

"The river really does divide the city in two. You only have to go along it to see the differences on each side.

"The Yarra does not have a lot of turbulence. It is a very restful thing to go down it by boat.

"We have found that the river has a calming effect on people and the action of the play acts against that."

"Breaking up in Balwyn" traces the fluctuating moods of a riverboat divorce party thrown by a lady-about-town from North Balwyn, Samantha Hart-Byrne.

Among the guests, invited and uninvited, are her Sydney filmmaker boyfriend, a psychiatrist, a member of the vice squad and her ex-husband, a noted tax minimiser.

If the success of "Storming" is an indicator, "Breaking" will attract many people who do not normally go to the theatre, according to Mark Shirrefs.

"We got a real cross-section. The tram show was almost completely booked out."

There were also some confused innocents who hailed a tram and got a theatre!

"This is a solid comedy. It's good entertainment, so we hope for much the same thing."

Unlike most theatres, the riverboat's audience will not be passive.

"People on the boat will be very much part of the action," Mark Shirrefs said, "but they won't be called on to sing songs or anything like that."

To simulate the low roof of the riverboat, a string has been erected about two metres above the floor of the cast's rehearsal centre at the old Canterbury Library.

Mark Shirrefs admits the confined space will create problems and he can't draw on the experience of other companies to overcome them.

Just as "Storming" was the first play performed on a tram, "Breaking up in Balwyn" will be the first performed on a Yarra riverboat.

The writer, Paul Davies, who has also managed to get a part in the play, is enthusiastic about the development of community theatre.

"The community theatre movement is almost totally a Victorian concept.

"What we are doing had its origins in the 60s.

"What we have got is a form of street theatre."

Street theatre Yarra-style "Breaking up in Balwyn," can be seen until April 10.

The production is part of the Moomba Festival and tickets can be bought at all Bass agencies.

This satire will break you up

'Breaking Up In Balwyn,' a satire on money, marriage and divorce is a play which take place on board a riverboat on the Yarra.

It is based on the short story of the same name which won second prize in the Syme Community Newspapers — City of Springvale short story competition.

Author Paul Davis, the resident playwright at Theatre Works, wrote last year's award winning story.

'Storming Mont Albert by Tram,' which was later performed by Theatre Works on board a moving tram with hilarious conswquences.

This years play has the same cast but this time the venue is the Yarra Princess riverboat which will wiend its way up the Yarra as events unfold.

The audience are the passengers/accomplices at a party hosted by one Samantha Hart-Byrne, a North Balwyn celebrity after she obtains her decree nisi from Michael Hart-Byrne, a corporation lawyer and well-known tax minister.

The play promises to do for divorces whgat Dimboola did for marriages.

Among the guest the audience will meet as they sail up river are Samantha and her boyfriend's psychiatrist. Serving drinks will be Zeeta Bleakville, a maid with silver service experience — but how much wallop does her punch really pack?

'Breaking Up In Balwyn' will be performed from Thursday 24 February to Sunday 10 April and the boat leaves from Princess Walk Landing, corner Batman Avenue, and Princes Bridge every weeknight at 8.,15 pm. On weekends it will leave form Princes Walk Landing at 5 pm except for 19,20 March, when it will leave at 3 pm.

Theatre Works show sold out

There is a glimmer of hope for those who didn't manage to get tickets to the Theatre Works' production "Breaking Up in Balwyn" — the season may be extended.

"Breaking Up" has proved a resounding success and has sold out till the end of its present season on April 10.

The play is a satire on money, marriage and divorce, and takes place on the Yarra Princess riverboat where the audience are guests of North Balwyn celebrity Samantha Hart-Byrne, who is celebrating her decree nisi.

Theatre Works administrator, Mr Martin Foot, said the group had been delighted at the reception given to its production — by both patrons and critics.

If the season is extended it will be for a maximum of two weeks. Tickets are $12.90, $6.90 concession and available from BASS outlets.

For inquiries call Theatre Works on 285 3339.

Divorce: a good excuse for a party

» ANGIE FOX

A few weeks shy of her 40th birthday in 2012, Sammie Black received her divorce papers in the mail and literally jumped around with elation.

She was so elated that she threw a "divorced and 40" cocktail party for her girlfriends, where they partied into the early hours.

It was "cathartic", says the communications consultant.

"I was extremely depressed in that marriage ... I felt like I was in a jail in that I wasn't free to be me. The reason why I wanted to celebrate was that it was the next chapter in my life and it was all looking good."

Black is not alone in choosing to celebrate her divorce. Like many trends it starts with celebrities. White Stripes singer Jack White and his model wife Karen Elson announced their divorce to friends via a divorce party invitation, while British media personality Katie Price threw a three-day divorce party in Ibiza after splitting from Australian singer Peter Andre.

The trend is rapidly growing in Australia, where more than 40 per cent of marriages end in divorce. Party planners are now staging divorce events that can be as elaborate as a wedding, replete with band, full bar and a divorce cake – with black icing.

Sydney psychologist Brett Stathis is in favour of the new industry. "It helps people to move on knowing that they have the support of their friends and that [divorce] is not something to be ashamed of."

Stathis speaks from experience. When he married in 2000, he never imagined his second wedding anniversary would become a "divorce-iversary". But nine months later his "rock-star" marriage disintegrated.

close friends to Sydney "lingerie" re Twin Peaks – a popular destination f nights – to celebrate his "new lease o

Last month Gwyneth Paltrow and front man Chris Martin provided the with a new cultural reference when t announced their "conscious uncoup Gone are the *Kramer vs Kramer*-sty tions of couples duking it out in cour might argue the announcement on F Goop blog was a way of controlling t

But the sentiment, to honourably tionship, still provides a new roadm those navigating the tricky terrain o particularly when children are invol

Black says she laughed out loud w heard the phrase "conscious uncoup "I can't imagine doing a joint stat anyone about my relationship break because we weren't too friendly dur it," she says. "If it is an amicable spli do that, and kudos to you."

Another woman, who asked not t named, said she was "blindsided" w husband cleaned out the home whil work. The protracted legal, financia tody proceedings were even more

When it was all over, she invite guests to a "freedom" party tha a spirit bar, live band and karao wasn't about him in any way. T no burning effig

It was about mo not man-bashi says. She even members of he husband's famil

"When you m marry a whole munity and a r it is the same divorce," she

---

```
WRK 679  event code     MOOMBA & THEATREWORKS     WRK679  event code
1129                      PRESENT ON THE
                   YARRA PRINCESS RIVERBOAT
GA  ADULT          BREAKING UP IN BALWYN          GA
sec.                                              sec./box
CAS  AVAC3        PRINCESS BRIDGE LANDING AQAVAC3
GEN  12.90  TUE 15TH MAR 1983 8.15PM GEN ADM
row  price                                        row
           GEN ADMISSON        ADULT    24FEB83
ADM  H24FEB  GA     GA-9       12.90    9
seat                                     seat
```

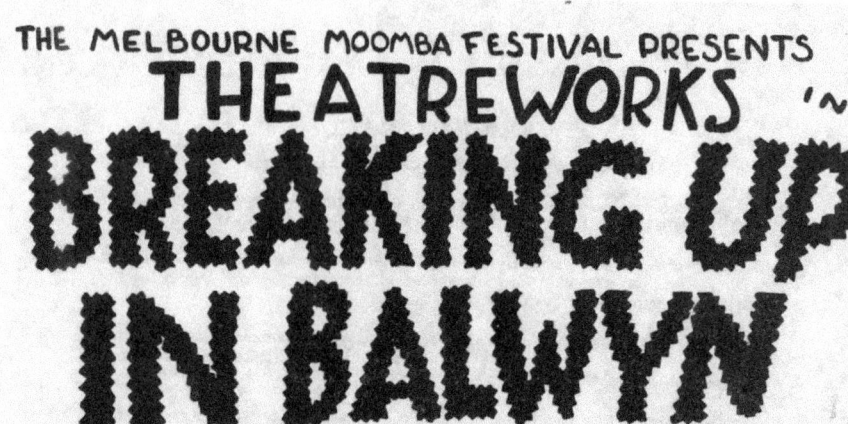

ILLUMINATORS:

Ivan Johnston – Performance Images

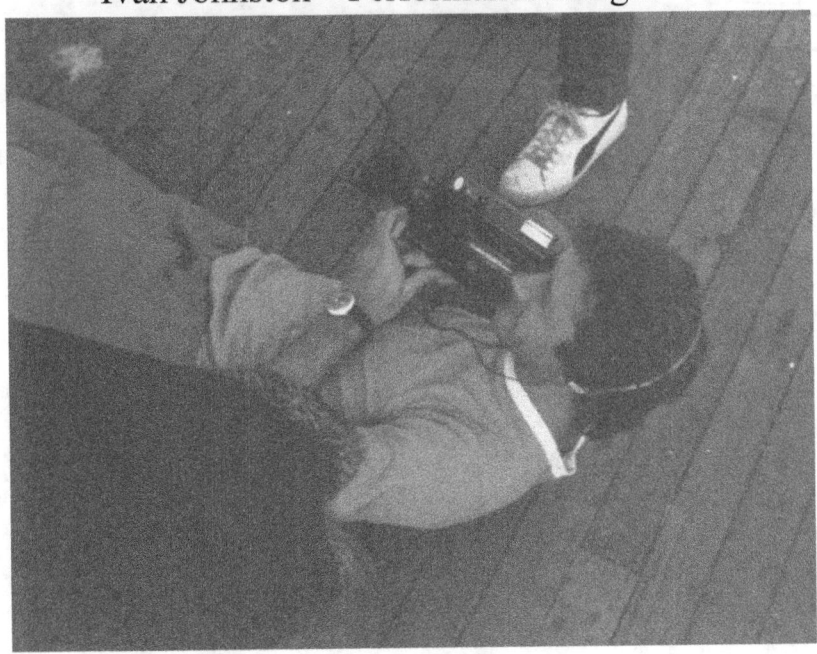

James Grant   Wedding images

Paul Davies is an award winning screenwriter, script editor and playwright who sharpened his quill on over a hundred episodes of Teledrama from classic Crawford series such as *Homicide* (1974-5), *The Box* (1975-76) *The Sullivans* (1976-78) and *Skyways* (1979), to *Rafferty's Rules* (1985), *Blue Heelers* (1997), *Pacific Drive* (1996), *Stingers* (1998-2003), *Something in the Air* (1999-2001) and *Headland* (2005). He also helped spark the site-specific performance revolution in Melbourne in the 1980s with TheatreWorks' production of his first play *Storming Mont Albert By Tram* (1982). What became known as *The Tram Show* played across a dozen years to packed trams in both Melbourne and Adelaide, travelling a total distance that would have taken the show halfway round the world.

TheTram Show's success lead to an outbreak of 'location theatre' in Melbourne throughout the 1980s including three other plays written to be performed in real places: *Breaking Up In Balwyn* (1983, on a riverboat), *Living Rooms* (1986, in an historic mansion) and *Full House/No Vacancies* (1989, in a boarding house).

These works became the subject of his book *Really Moving Drama*. Both *The Tram Show* and *On Shifting Sandshoes* (1988) were awarded AWGIES, along with *Return of The Prodigal* (2000) an episode of *Something In The Air* (ABC). Paul co-wrote the feature *Neil Lynn* with David Baker in 1984, and the docu-fiction *Exits* (1980) with Pat Laughren and Carolyn Howard. Paul has also worked on the scripts of John Hughes' documentaries, *Traps* (1984), *All That Is Solid* (1985), and *One Way Street (Fragments for Walter Benjamin)* (1991). As well as Rosie Jones' *Holy Rollers* (2001) and Pat Laughren's *Red Ted And the Great Depression* (1992).

The novel, *33 Postcards From Heaven* was published by Gondwana Press in 2005. Numerous articles, reviews, stories and interviews have been published in *Metro, Cinema Papers, Cantrill's Filmnotes, Australasian Drama Studies, Community Theatre In Australia, The Macquarie Companion to the Australian Media* and *Theatre Research International* (Cambridge University). Paul has also given courses in literature and creative writing at various colleges and universities including: Southern Cross, James Cook and Melbourne State.

www.ingramcontent.com/pod-product-compliance
Lightning Source LLC
Chambersburg PA
CBHW050305010526
44107CB00055B/2112